IT WAS NOTHING!

Phyllis Muriel Smith

iUniverse, Inc.
New York   Bloomington

IT WAS NOTHING!

iUniverse books may be ordered through booksellers or by contacting:

iUniverse
1663 Liberty Drive
Bloomington, IN 47403
www.iuniverse.com
1-800-Authors (1-800-288-4677)

Because of the dynamic nature of the Internet, any Web addresses or links contained in this book may have changed since publication and may no longer be valid.

ISBN: 978-1-4502-1875-7 (sc)
ISBN: 978-1-4502-1876-4 (dj)
ISBN: 978-1-4502-1877-1 (ebk)

Printed in the United States of America

iUniverse rev. date: 4/8/2010

The following is several mini-novels, and a collection of stories with pictures, along with proof positive that the Smith family really existed, who they were, and much, much more. Phyllis Smith loved to write as much as she loved to live. At the end of her life it was confirmed by her son, Punch, that only one regret existed, only one unaccomplished task remained, and that was a small undertaking that he would not allow to haunt him. So after many years and countless rejection slips, the words of Phyllis M. Smith will be published and will remain in libraries, book stands and even in bathrooms through out the world.

Contents

Chapter 1

IT WAS NOTHING

A Book By, For and About Phyllis Smith

Editor's Notes

Phyllis died on July 7, 2009 in Charleston, SC. She was ready to "go to the other side", as she told Punch several times during her last 18 months, while residing comfortably at The Palms of Mount Pleasant. Many family members had gathered in Charleston the previous September to celebrate her 90th. They found her alert and happy with her wry sense of humor still intact, but more fragile and dependent. She died mostly of old age, without suffering, and thanks to the gifted nurses at Hospice with dignity and at peace. A Celebration of Life service was held in the "Quiet Corner" of Connecticut that August attended by over 80 family and friends.

Born in Canada to parents who drifted apart early, Phyllis was raised in Providence by her mother, Ida Lee, a solemn school teacher and a benevolent great uncle, David, during the depression. At 17, fresh out of high school, she met a handsome, athletic widower and his three children at camp on the Rhode Island shore. She married Norm at 18 and the journey began.

Setting up a household in Pennsylvania for five, as a teacher/coaches' wife, sending her husband off to WWII, birthing her own two boys, joining the Junior League, relocating to Connecticut to be closer to their aging mothers, beating cancer and heart challenges, volunteering for the Democratic Party, etc., etc.

Along the way, she formed many lasting friendships, published articles about a lot of funny family adventures, gave to the community, kept a beautiful home, full of books and antiques, tended a colorful garden, enjoyed her extended family, entertained easily, cooked superbly, and led a full and active life. Her story, we believe, is captured in the pages of eclectic documents that follow.

Phyllis always dreamed of publishing her articles, but somehow never got around to it. We are proud to produce this "book" in her memory.

Punch and Clay Smith February 2010

Rejection Slips

Phyllis kept the regret notices from various publications for her numerous submitted articles. Scattered throughout her files were short notes to herself, bemoaning the thought that her book would never ever be published. The formal rejections however, never deterred her passion to keep writing. Here are just a few of the actual short response letters that would have discouraged most writers:

THIS WEEK MAGAZINE 420 LEXINGTON AVENUE, NEW YORK, N.Y.

We have read the enclosed contribution with interest, and regret that it is not quite suited to the needs of THIS WEEK. The large number of manuscripts we receive makes it impossible to explain in a personal letter our reasons for returning yours, but we thank you for letting us see it.

William I. Nichols
Editor

WOMAN'S DAY MAGAZINE
19 WEST 44TH STREET . NEW YOR CITY 36

We are sorry the enclosed material is not suited to our needs. While the manuscripts we receive are too numerous to allow individual criticism, we want you to know that yours received careful consideration.

Thank you for letting us review it.
THE EDITORS

572 Madison Ave., New York 22
HOUSE BEAUTIFUL MAGAZINE
Telephone Plaza 1-1200

October 1, 1958

Mrs. Phyllis M. Smith
Sunnybank Farm
East Woodstock, Conn.

Dear Mrs. Smith:

Thank you for submitting "Push Button Paradise" for our consideration. You have written an amusing piece, but I am afraid it does not fall with our present editorial needs.

I am returning your article with our thanks for thinking of us.

Cordially,
Marianne Wentworth
Assistant to the Editor

THE SMITH FAMILY

Phyllis' parents - Ida Lee Noble, born in Abilene, Kansas in April 1880, and Martin James Oxley, born in Chimney Corner, Nova Scotia in August 1881. They were married in Humboldt, Saskatchewan in July 1916. Martin died Calgary, Alberta in November 1938. Ida Lee died in Providence, RI, in December 1953.

Norm's parents – Flora Jane Wade, born in Chepachet, RI, in May 1878 and Robert Lewis Smith, born in Glocester, RI, in August 1876. They were married in May 1897 in Putnam, Connecticut. Robert died in Providence, RI, in April 1958. Flora died in Chepachet, RI, in September 1966.

PHYLLIS MURIEL SMITH

Phyllis – born September 5, 1918 in Tessier, Saskatchewan, Canada to Martin James and Ida Lee Oxley. Martin was a grain buyer and Ida Lee, a school teacher. Her parents were estranged for most of their marriage. Phyllis, and her brother Ken, one year older, moved along with their mother, to Providence to live with their benevolent Uncle David. She married Norman in June 1937. They lived in the Wyoming Valley of Pennsylvania until 1950 when they moved to northeast Connecticut to be close to their aging mothers who lived near by in Rhode Island as an American citizen. She was naturalized in 1962. Phyllis resided in the "Quiet Corner" until 2007 when she relocated to the Charleston, SC area. A courageous cancer survivor, she died in Hospice on July 7, 2009, age 90. The details of her eventful life reside in this compilation of many documents written by, to, and about her.

NORMAN WADE SMITH

Born in Chepachet, Rhode Island on January 13, 1902, to Flore Wade and Robert Lee Smith. The second eldest of seven children. He attended Providence Technical High School, Dean Academy, including earning 9 letters in college football, basketball, and baseball. He held post graduate degrees from Springfield College and Harvard University. He married Helen Burdick, his college sweetheart, right after graduation in 1925, and they had Bob, Norma and Wade. Helen died suddenly and tragically in 1933, as mentioned in Wade's bio. He married Phyllis in 1937 and they had Punch and Keith. He was a coach and professor at Wyoming Seminary from 1926 until being called to active duty with the Army in 1941, to plan and implement the new concept of Special Services. He was the senior Morale Officer on Patton's staff, participating in the North Africa, the Sicilian and the Naples, Foggia campaigns, and was wounded in 1943, and returned to duty stateside. He was discharged as a Colonel in 1947, returning to duty this time as Athletic Director. The family moved to Connecticut in 1950, as mentioned in Phyllis' bio. He subsequently held positions in teaching and coaching at a variety of prep schools, summer camps and resorts, namely The Rectory School – 10 years, Marianapolis Prep School – 20 years, Jug End Barn, Spring Lake Ranch – 8 summers and Camp Indian Acre – 18 summers. He was universally loved and respected by his students/athletes, who nicknamed him the "Gen" in honor of his military service and leadership ability. He was a fascinating story teller, and stand-up speaker, entertaining various audiences with his keen wit and huge smile for over 50 years. He was a member of the Sports Trail Century Club for coaches for 1000 victories, in 1964, and subsequently won another 85 before retiring for good. He died in the Veteran's Hospital in Newington, Connecticut in November 1977, at age 75.

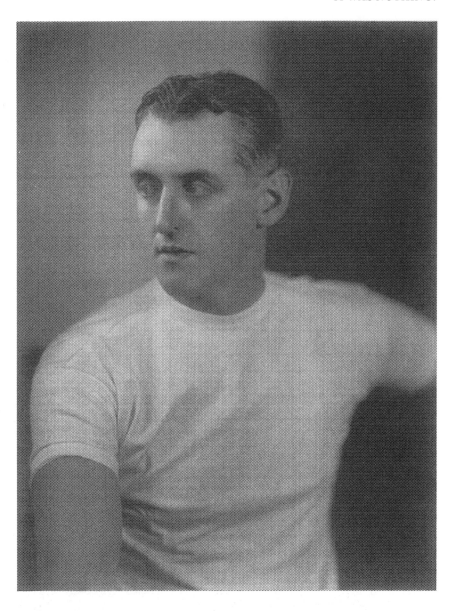

The General in his early years

COLONEL ROBERT N SMITH USMC

The Marine Corps Officer is a leader, a warrior and an upstanding citizen, instilled with the special trust and confidence of our nation to lead her expeditionary forces. Robert (Bob) Smith was, and will always be, one of them.

Bob prepped for the Naval Academy at Wyoming Seminary in Kingston, PA. At Wyoming he was a three year letterman who captained the football team, as well as being president of his class. Bob entered the Naval Academy in 1944. He was a member of the football team and Regimental Commander. Bob graduated in 1948, and was commissioned as a Marine officer. He played end on the Quantico football team and was selected twice to All-Marine teams.

Bob earned his wings in 1952. He saw extensive carrier duty aboard Wright, Coral Sea and Forrestal; flying Corsairs, AD's, the F-8 and the F-4B. He also served in various staff positions including the staff of the Commander Sixth Fleet. On August 19, 1969 Lt. Col. Robert N. Smith and his RIO, Capt. John N. Flanigan departed DaNang in their F4B Phantom fighter/bomber jet aircraft to fly escort on a photo reconnaissance mission just north of the Demilitarized Zone. Bob's aircraft made one run over the target, and then he and the other aircraft separated, but Bob never returned for the second run and contact was never reestablished. The area in which they were last seen, about 5 miles east of the city of Ninh Linh in Quang Binh Province, North Vietnam was known to be heavily defended. Memorial services were held for Bob at Arlington National Cemetery, his marker is in the MIA section. Bob's name is also on "The Wall". Maya Lin, the young architect who designed the Vietnam Memorial Wall grew up in Athens, Ohio, and was a neighbor of Bob's widow, Jane.

NORMA SMITH BOND

in April, 1928, the second child of Helen and Norm, and the only girl. Her own mother died when she was just 5 years old and was 9 when Norm married Phyllis. Norma graduated from Wyoming Seminary and the Geisinger School of Nursing. Like Norm's four sons, Norma was a fine athlete, and served in the military as an Army nurse for 3 years, where she met her husband, Sam Bond. They had one son, Jeffrey, who has unfortunately dropped out of site. Norma died of cancer in November 1990. The memorial message from the Prince Georges Hospital Center, see below, confirms that Norma was a dedicated, compassionate and skilled professional, who took great pride in her work, and loved teaching others. She was a devoted wife to her husband Sam, a wounded veteran of the Korean conflict, and printer, who died in 1999. We continue to try to locate Jeff.

DECEMBER 1990   PRINCE GEORGE'S HOSPITAL CENTER

In Loving Memory

Norma Bond

1928–1990

Norma Bond, R.N., one of Prince George's Hospital Center's most endearing employees passed away on Sunday, November 4th at the Hospital Center.

Norma, a native of Connecticut, graduated from Geisinger Medical Center, School of Nursing in Danville, Pennsylvania. She served as an Army nurse from 1950-1952. Afterwards, she joined the Prince George's Hospital Center staff in 1953.

In her 37 years at the Prince George's Hospital Center, Norma was an evening nursing supervisor, taught at the Hospital Center's School of Practical Nursing, and was the Nursing Standards Coordinator.

Over 175 friends, family members and co-workers at-

tended a memorial service on Friday, November 9th in the Hospital Center's auditorium. The ceremony was very touching as everyone was able to share stories about what a lovely and life enriching human being Norma was and still is in the hearts of many.

"Norma was a friendly and familiar face around the Hospital Center and she always thought of Prince George's Hospital Center as her family," says Rose Bartosevich, R.N., Administrative Coordinator, and good friend of Norma's.

A memorial fund in Norma's memory has been established by the Prince George's Hospital Center Foundation, Inc. The monies collected will be used for a scholarship for nursing students. Anyone interested in contributing to the memorial fund should contact the Foundation office at 618-3980.

Norma Bond was more than an employee for 37 years, she was a good friend to many.

DONALD WADE SMITH

Born in March 1930 in Kingston, Pennsylvania. He graduated from Wyoming Seminary and the U.S. Coast Guard Academy in 1953. He spent a full career in the Coast Guard, covering many diverse and interesting assignments, including CO of the Port of Philadelphia, and retired as a Captain, after 24 years. He married Barbara right after graduation, and they had four children, David, Carol, Peter and Heidi. After retirement, Wade worked from Travelers Insurance in New Orleans. He was married to Edith for several years. After her death, Wade married Sally. They are retired and live in Bluffton, South Carolina.

NORMAN WADE SMITH , JR. "PUNCH"

Born May 16, 1942 in Kingston, Pennsylvania. Graduated from Rectory School, Pomfret School and Cornell University. Married Nancy in 1964. Have three daughters, Jennifer, Kelly and Erin, and six grandchildren. Was a Marine in RVN, retired as a Colonel after 4 years active duty, and 24 in the Reserves. Worked 40 years for several private companies, ABEX, American Hospital Supply, Norton, Dixie Industrial, and Cameron & Barkley, as a Salesman, Sales Trainer, but mostly as a Sales Manager and Regional VP. The Punch Smith families all live in Mount Pleasant, South Carolina.

KEITH LEE SMITH

Born July 22, 1944 in Kingston, Pa. Graduated from Rectory School, Marianapolis Prep School, and Clemson University. He played football and was commissioned through the ROTC program as an Army officer. He served 3 years active as a "tanker". He and Carolyn had two sons, Shane and Spencer, who now live in California. He married Miranda in 1977, and had a daughter, Sara, and a son, Philip, who live in Connecticut. Keith worked as a Salesman and Sales Manager for several companies, including Norton, North and Scott, from whom he retired in 2009. He and Miranda live in South Woodstock, Ct., and tend to many quite senior animals.

CHAPTER 2

Phyllis's Early Years

These are excerpts from a short autobiography Wade wrote at the insistence of his children, so they would understand his childhood, and theirs also. The "Early Years" mentions the sad, untimely passing of Norm's first wife Helen, and how Wade was somewhat responsible for Phyllis and Norm meeting. This period covers from 1930, when Wade was born, through 1943, when matriculated at Wyoming Seminary, where Norm taught and coached before and after his active duty during WWII, and Bob and Norma graduating.

EARLY YEARS

I was born on March 11, 1930, in the Nesbitt Hospital, Kingston, PA., time of day unknown. My father was Norman Wade Smith, a school teacher and coach at a private prep school, Wyoming Seminary in Kingston, PA. My mother was a housewife. I had an older brother, Robert Norman Smith, who is four years my senior and an older sister, Norma Burdick Smith, who is two years older. We lived in a first floor faculty apartment in the boy's dorm. Dad taught various math subjects and was a coach of football, basketball, and baseball. The apartment had no kitchen or dining room as we ate our meals in the school dining room.

These tables were round and with ten chairs. Each table was headed by a teacher and his family, the remaining seats were taken by students. Two other teacher families had boys my age and we became playmates. During the school year we lived in the dorm, in the summer Dad rented a cottage at Bonnet Shores at the ocean front in Rhode Island nearby my grandparents on my mother's side. My father's parents lived in Providence, RI.

my first recollection of life was at Bonnet Shores. I remember the cottage, the path going down the hill to the beach, playing on the beach and having lunch with the family. The food always tasted like sand. I was not much for going in the water and was known as the "sand flea". I also remember the inside of the cottage. My bed was inside the window to the closed-in porch. At three years, I was still a bed wetter. One morning I woke up to a wet bed. My Dad was sitting on the day bed which was on the porch on the other side of the window. I crawled through the window and told Dad about the wet bed just as my mother discovered it. Dad hid me under the day bed and to this day, I can remember lying there and seeing her legs passing back and forth as she was looking for me. Fortunately, I don't remember the ending of this incident. Later that month, I remember a morning when my grandparents were there along with some others, they kept passing in and out of my mother's bedroom. There was no door, just a curtain and I can still see the people rushing around, and mother died that August day, 1933 of a streptococcus throat. There were no miracle drugs, no antibiotics, and no cure. She was buried in a cemetery in Kingston, RI near Grandpa Burdick's home. I do not remember the funeral, however I have seen a picture of the three Smith kids standing at her fresh dug grave. The big family headstone says, Burdick, mom's name is carved on the back with the date of her birth and death.

The next summer after my mother's death, we did not return to Bonnet Shores, Dad had found a summer camp on Worden Pond, near my grandparent's home in Kingston, RI. The pond was about 10 miles in circumference, heavily wooded along the shores with cottages widely spaced between one hundred yards to a quarter mile. You could not see the neighbors from ours. The house was about fifty yards back form the water, and about two hundred yards in front of the county road. The entrance road was dirt loaded with rocks and filled with potholes. No electricity, no heat, no bathroom. Kerosene lamps were used for light, an ice box on the back porch for storage of foods, (one summer a skunk took to living under the ice box), and a two hole outhouse in the back yard. There was a rickety, wooden dock with a rowboat provided by the owner. I loved it here, just perfect for a little kid. I went bare foot most of the time, played mostly by myself. Went swimming in the shallow water, rowed the boat, played with my cars/trucks in the dirt, built a log cabin from downed trees, etc. When the wind blew down the lake, us kids would row the boat up wind, open the umbrella and sail to the other end. One summer, someone gave us an old kayak and Dad's cousin, who owned a race track, loaned us a pony named Jackie. She would transport the pony in the back seat of an old Packard, along with several of her kids. Jackie got loose one night and ran away. We found him about five miles down the road in a farmer's field. We really didn't like the pony, so one summer was enough. One rainy day, Norma would blackmail me into playing dolls. Not a guy's thing. Some mornings Dad made us box (like in boxing) before breakfast. Everybody beat me up. Norma would beat up Bob. She would make him laugh so hard with her windmill style of punching that he couldn't punch back. The family made a lot of day trips to the beach, fisherman's wharf, grandmas, the cemetery, the Rhode Island State College campus to watch football practice. The college was at Kingston, my grandpa worked there and his house adjoined the campus on the north. Both my mother and father graduated from State in 1925. Grandpa was a professor in the College of Agriculture, head of the Department of Maintenance and grounds, and head of the Farm and Dairy Barn. Some days I was allowed to travel around with him. He had a driver who drove and old beat up pickup truck. The third week in August was always the Rhode Island State Fair, the fairgrounds was only five miles from our camp. We would go every day and stay until dark. These were fun days for me. I just loved the college farm, especially the dairy barn.

The summer of 1934 I found my way through the woods to the next cabin, which really was a log cabin. It was occupied by Sam and Stella Brown, in my eyes an old couple. Stella took a liking to me and several days each week, I would walk through the woods to her place and she would take me swimming, in fact she taught me how to swim. One day, there was a teenage girl there who was introduced as Phyllis Oxley, the Brown's niece. The three of us made a day of swimming, playing games and eating. That afternoon a thunderstorm passed through and darkness fell before I could go home. Mrs. Brown and Phyllis, with flashlights in hand, walked me to my cottage. Grandma Smith invited them in for a visit. I guess that Dad had an eye for that teenage girl because every day for the next few weeks he would send me to the Brown's and then come over to fetch me. Phyllis was sixteen and a junior in high school. Soon the dating started. Phyllis lived with her mother in Providence, Rhode Island. Her parents were married, however her father lived in Canada, and would show up infrequently for visits. I remember that he always wore a hat, inside and out, even in the bathroom.

The summer of 1937, Dad and Phyllis were married somewhere in Maine, no family members in attendance. Norma and I stayed with the Burdick's and I put up a fuss when Dad left because I wanted to tag along. They honeymooned at a place called the Desert of Maine. Phyllis moved in and Grandma Smith moved out. I am sure to grandmother's delight. Virginia went with her mother.

We returned to our Huntsville farm house that September, but Phyllis didn't take to the surroundings, and within a month or so we moved to a nice house in Shavertown. Phyllis purchased a lot of new furniture and a radio, never had a radio before. Now we could listen to the kids programs after school and the comedy shows Sunday night. The elementary school was only a quarter mile from the house, no buses, everybody walked, lots of kids, and plenty of stuff for me to do. There was a mom and pop food store next door. Sometimes after school the owner would hire me to help make deliveries to local residences. I would get paid in candy and sodas. There was a lumber yard to our back, and I would play in the stacks of lumber until one Saturday, when the owner caught me and told me to stay off his property. Hills were all around, so sled riding in the winter was easy. I also remember going door to door selling chances for a chocolate Easter egg. I was not a salesman, and I didn't care for sales. In fact, I turned in the money and kept the egg for myself.

The next year we moved to Trucksville, rented a house from Dad's friend and guess what, I got to go to the new school built from the ashes of the old school that burned down. Only drawback, the school was about three miles away and all the kids had to walk. It was tough in the winter. The new house was half way up a steep hill, just across the street from a three acre grass lot behind the Catholic Church, perfect place to play ball and just horse around. Sometimes the young priests would come and join us. I remember a young girl in our group of kids who walked together, took a liking to me. She said it was a leap year and girls carried the boy's books. That was okay with me. Then one afternoon, I was playing in the field across the street near her house. She called to me and said she wanted to show me something in her garage. Innocent me, I went in and low and behold, she threw her arms around me and started kissing. At nine years old boys didn't do that kind of thing, and that was the end of that friendship. Another thing, at Christmas the parents in this neighborhood put up the tree on Christmas Eve. We didn't know that and after our tree went up on about the twentieth, every mother on the street was calling wondering what in tarnation we were doing around here, Santa brought the tree. Ever hear of such a thing? It was nice going to a brand new school, really modern for the times. I was still not much of a student, but a great baseball player. Recess was my thing. Our family had made many friendships around this town and life was great. We still went to church in Huntsville by car.

Dad had leased this house for only a year, and Phyllis had been looking for something to buy. They found an old house with a barn in the Huntsville area, just below the dam which holds back water from a high reservoir. The spillway ran along the road just across from our new house. You could hear the water flow when the doors and windows were open. Some old lady had lived in this place for years.

Since our house was inside the Jackson Township line, I was to attend the one room school house which was about a two mile walk. One teacher for eight grades, I was in sixth and there were four students at this level. There was a farm next door and the farmer's son, Frankie was my agent. He was required by his father to work on the farm, no time to play. I even had my own cow to milk, her name was June and she was easy to milk.

In the spring during planting and in the fall at harvest, the farmer would hire me for a one dollar a day, plus my noon meal. After a year or two, I drove the mule team when we picked up hay and corn. One day when Frankie was away, the farmer told me to go to the barn and harness the mules. One mule, Jack, was nice, the other, Jerry, he was not so happy to see me, and tried to kick me with his rear leg. As I moved forward along his side to avoid the kick, he turned his head and bit me in the back. All he got was a mouth full of clothing, and I was out of there. The farmer got a big laugh. Work on the farm was hard, this farmer just barely made a living. In the winter, when there was snow on the ground, the animals had to be attended to, cows milked twice a day, but there was idle time which was filled by hauling coal to the local homes directly from the mines. On some Saturday mornings, I would make coal trips. All in all, I enjoyed working on the farm, to Phyllis' dismay. It seemed to her that I was never home and when I did come home, I smelled like a stinking barnyard. Now, this is where and when I learned all about the "birds and the bees". My job was to help the bull by holding the cow's tail. I never told Phyllis, I am sure she would have disapproved. My final report card from that one-room school was all A's and B's. Dad announced that I was not an A/B student and the next year he would arrange with the same principal at Lehman School for me to attend that school. To catch the Lehman bus, all I had to do was walk about one hundred yards up the hill, which was over the Township line into Lehman.

The war had started in Europe and early in September 1939, the US had remained neutral, however it was certain that we would be involved. The draft had started and the reserves activated. Dad was a Captain in the Army reserves and was called to duty the summer of 1940 and assigned to the Aberdeen Proving Grounds, Aberdeen, MD. The Japs had attacked Pearl Harbor Naval Base and other military bases in Oahu, Hawaii, and the US declared war against Japan and Germany. I remember that day of December 7th, 1941 like it was only last year. The country went on war alert, and scary times were to follow. Dad had word that he would go to England to teach hand to hand combat to the British Commandos, so the family went to live in Huntsville. Phyllis was with child and wanted to be home for the birth. Punch arrived May 16, 1942.

Norma and Bob were already borders at Wyoming Seminary and I started school at Lehman. I liked being home in Huntsville, back to my old friends, the farm next door, the church activities, my bicycle, my territory.

Several weeks after Punch was born, Dad shipped out to England. In November of 1942, the Americans landed in Morocco and Algeria during Operations Torch. Dad was under the command of General Patton. This Army group drove the Germans east. This was the first test for the Americans, and not all the fighting went well. At Kasserine Pass our troops took a licking and Dad was wounded. He was first evacuated to England, then to an Army hospital at Fort Polk, LC. After he recuperated, he was transferred to an army facility near Ashville, North Carolina. Phyllis and Punch went down there, and that summer, Phyllis put me up with a family friend at his brother's chicken farm and apple orchard. The living area was in the front of the chicken barn. No women in this family, only two brothers and they didn't know what to do with this young kid. They worked me like a slave with no pay, just board. They called Phyllis and now I was a border at the Nuss'. That fall I attended the eighth grade at Lehman. Living with the Nuss family was great, they were like Mom and Dad to me with three boy playmates built in. Phyllis tells the story that one day while walking down the street in Ashville, they met the Duke and Duchess of Windsor. The Duchess patted Punch's head and said, "What a cute little fellow".

Dad was transferred to Washington, DC to be in charge of special services in the Army. This was great duty for dad, it was like being in Heaven. He would gather all the pro football players in one camp, form a team and go around beating up on teams from other military bases and college teams. In the winter, he would do the same for basketball and in the spring, baseball.

In the spring of 1943, I took the entrance examination for Wyoming Seminary. All children of the faculty passed regardless of the test results. So that September I would be attending school at Seminary as a boarder, paying my way with a working scholarship, waiting on tables in the dining room.

Chapter 3

THREE ACRES
And Six Dependents

FROM PILLER TO POST

BY MRS. T.M.B. HICKS, JR.

Hats off to Phyllis, she's writing an exuberant autobiography with no holds barred, and it makes amusing reading.

"THREE ACRES" isn't a column, nor should it be assayed as such. It is the beginning of a book which when completed will undoubtedly find a publisher, for though it is suggestive in its treatment of "The Egg and I", it is far more cleverly written. It is breezy in spots, but life is breezy at times, and a person who can take everything as it comes with a grain of salt and with the tongue in the cheek, has gone a long way toward making a bargain with the future.

every writer should resign himself with his first published word to the fact that it is impossible to please everybody. Break into print, and there you are, a handy target. That's the price for expressing yourself, a lifelong residence in a glass house with not enough Venetian blinds to go around.

As a general rule, if you approach writing or life with the ambition of giving no offense and pleasing everybody, you give offense where none was intended, and you please nobody, not even yourself. If you don't achieve either of these distinctions, you take shape in the local mind as a vague and formless wrath, entirely lacking in personality.

You can't win. I remember with wry amusement that a local merchant took exception to my account of a harmless thumbing through the pages of a Sears Roebuck catalogue in search of some luxury item that would amount to precisely ten dollars, postage included, ten dollars being the exact amount of binge money with no strings attached to it, which was mine to spend. The fact that the money was never spent at all, but laid philosophically aside to finance an umbrella for a rainy day, didn't figure in the argument, which was that if Mrs. Hicks was not going to spend ten dollars, she ought to not spend it rummaging through a local store to the confusion of the clerks and the ruination of the shelf arrangements instead of not spending it comfortably in front of the fire with her feet elevated to the top of the Franklin stove and the shoulder blades comforted with cushions.

After all the proof of the pudding, etc. etc. I note that the readers who profess to be the most deeply disturbed about the biological inferences in "Three Acres" are the very ones who dive most earnestly for the second page of the Post in order not to miss anything.

And I'm now sitting back and waiting for reverberations.

Naming My Book

I have always had a secret loathing for authors who name books and then fail in one way or another to explain their titles. H. Allen Smith (no relation) is certainly a past master at giving screwy titles, but he at least goes into detail as to how he arrived at the names for his little gems of American literature. Take his book "Rhubarb" for instance. Upon seeing that title, I immediately thought of that ugly green herb which grows so profusely around outhouses in nasty old farmyards. Perhaps twelve million fellow Americans would have thought the same thing if author Smith had not enlightened us.

However, I do feel that the artist who designed the jacket for "Rhubarb" stole a bit of H. Allen's thunder. That ingenious illustrator was faced with the grueling ordeal of designing a cover for a book whose main character was a cat. How or when the idea for the book jacket fermented in the artist's mind, I have no knowledge, but the result was the most senile looking old tomcat you ever laid eyes on. I have no doubt that the artist lived on steak for six months after from the money earned sketching that cat, and that's the part that hurts.

In selecting the title of "Three Acres and Six Dependents" I realize I have created an illustrator's nightmare. I wonder what the person who drew the cat could to with that name. Just in case it proves impossible to illustrate, I had better explain where I got the title. Eight years ago when we joined the back to the soil movement, we found ourselves living in a dilapidated old farmhouse surrounded by three acres of ground we could, but didn't care to call our own. If there had been any old soil lying around the joint, it would have been thoroughly eroded. It was the kind of place that even Louis Bromfield couldn't redeem.

I was still in the first throes of this return to the land when I saw an ad in the "New York Times" concerning a young couple who had thrown discretion to the winds and settled on an acre of their own. At the end of the first year they had everything on that small plot of earth you could think of. I don't recall a Ferris wheel being mentioned, but outside of that, the acre was complete. These eager beavers were really delighted that they had renounced life in a stuffy city apartment and started anew in the wilds of Connecticut. Their life soon evolved into a mad dash from a chicken coop to barn to deepfreeze, and they adored every moment of it. The one time they sat down they whipped up an intriguing little handbook for people like us to read and drool over. For the meager sum of one dollar, they would mail you a copy of their formula for killing yourself in a year's time, while your husband dashed into business each day then raced home to devour all the eggs you had gathered, the beans you had hoed, plus a large chunk of calf you had fattened. The gist of the whole thing was that you could have one acre and independence, plus anticipating your wife's untimely death. I showed the ad to my husband and asked if he thought we should send for the book. "Hell, no," he said, "I'm going to write a book myself, and call it "Three Acres and Six Dependents." That was eight years, and one war ago and, I have given Norm up as a writer. I asked him the other day, when he was going to start on his great novel and he said, "Don't you think I had better read a book before I write one?"

Now that H. Allen Smith has killed the novel form in America, it is safe for other citizens to chain themselves to typewriters and write about most anything that occurs to them. When I think back on what H. Allen hauled out of a cheese box, wedged between two bindings then sold for a book, I have no complexes, whatsoever. I know what follows will undoubtedly smell, but as one Smith to another, who cares?

LOVES AWAKENING

Not too long ago, I read in the paper that most marriages, if they survive, end up in a beautiful friendship. In looking back over the past eleven years, I am more or less in accord with that statement.

I met Norm, a widower of two years and father of three children, late in the summer of 1935. I was fresh out of Girl Scout camp and simply lousy with information on how to light fires without matches, how to tie knots, and last but not least, how to make shore in an overturned canoe. I might add that this type of knowledge was a complete loss once I met Norm. It would be unfair to say that Norm ended the career of a potential Juliet Lowe, but he certainly helped. For five long years, I had been an avid scout. I was covered with merit badges and carried enough equipment around on my belt to tire a mule; but I loved every minute of it.

That summer, however, I had become a wee bit cynical. "Big Chief", the head of the camp, a sexless creature with years of scouting to her credit, had decided to run the place like an Indian reservation instead of a Girl Scout camp. The tents were referred to as teepees, the counselors were given Indian names, and as result our teepee became the headquarters for all un-Indian-like activities. I had become the undisputed leader of our group when I refused to call our junior counselor, "Pocahontas". The unfortunate girl was a squat blond plagued with an uncooperative thyroid and I simply could not bring myself to call her "Pocahontas". My just punishment was another day of latrine duty.

Two days later my position as leader was threatened by a freckle-faced inmate of our teepee. "Freckles" had almost succeeded in drowning Pocahontas during life saving class that morning. Unfortunately, I had not been a witness to the joyous spectacle, as I was busy at the latrines.

My best friend brought me the news fresh from the waterfront and we two decided that it was time for me to do something equally daring.

Every morning before taps, we gathered around an open fire and sang songs. Of course with the new regime, the campfire of old had been named council fire and "Big Chief" held sway there every evening. On the night that I refer to, "Big Chief" was in fine spirits. Earlier in the day, she and the eunuch who tended the vegetable garden had found an old arrow head; so naturally she was greatly enthused and wanted everybody out for archery practice early the next morning. My friend and I sat there thinking over the possibilities of poisoned arrows with sadistic grins on our faces. Soon it was nine o'clock and we were rushed off to bed, and supposedly to sleep.

After fifteen minutes of agonizing silence and forced snoring, we could usually convince Pocahontas that we were asleep and she would slink away in the shadows and join her fellow counselors at the dying fire. That was when our day began. Our good mothers kept us supplied with cakes, cookies, and candy, so we gorged ourselves with sweets and thought up deviltry for the following day.

We all more or less wondered what the fair Indian maidens talked about after we had gone to bed, so I was appointed a committee of one to find out. The idea was too revolutionary that I slipped into my moccasins, and sallied forth leaving instructions for no one to fall asleep until I returned. I flitted through the woods as quietly as I could then crawled on my stomach to get close enough to hear the conversation. The topic under discussion was what measures would be taken in case some unwary male should stumble into that hot-bed of virginity. The girls all pledged to defend our honor in case something like that happened; but from the expression on "Big Chief's" face, I could tell she was hopeful her teepee would be the first one in the path of rape. I crawled quietly away, and had just started my mad dash to safety when a blood curdling scream filled the air. The gardener was taking a little stroll and I crashed smack into him. In a second we were surrounded by disappointed females and I was marched off to "Big Chief's" teepee to explain themeaning of such actions. I had visions of "Big Chief" scalping me, then wandering around the reservation next day with my mousy brown scalp dangling from her favorite Indian beaded belt. I hoped my friends would realize I had died for a good cause, and let "Freckles" take over until she met with a similar fate.

"Big Chief" stormed around her wigwam and ordered me off of the grounds the first thing in the morning. I explained that Mother was in Greenland giving her unsolicited approval of what Sir Wilfred Grenfell had done for the Eskimos, and that no one was at our home in Providence. My dear brother was giving his all to the Boy Scouts at Camp Yawgoo; so I casually suggested that I could join my aunt and uncle who had a cabin on a pond two miles from the Girl Scout camp.

The next morning I departed in disgrace and it didn't help matters any to have my uncle ask "Big Chief" if she was the head squaw when he called for me.

One day shortly after, I took a walk in the woods around my uncle's cabin and came across the Smith tribe who were living in the camp next to ours. Norm claims it was love at first sight as I emerged from their privy in my Girl Scout shorts. He was trying to start a fire in an outdoor fireplace and I could tell from the manner he's going about that he had never been a Boy Scout. I sauntered over and asked without benefit of an introduction, "Do you know the right way to start a fire?" He glanced up with a twinkle in his eye and said, "I always take two Girl Scouts and rub them together," and my heart stood still.

The Smith – A Mighty Man

Being the only Girl Scout within sight and smelling distance, I saw I was in no immediate danger, so I sat down on a nearby rock and eyed our new neighbor. He was tall, slim, gray-haired, and obviously not a victim of pyromania. You could tell at a glance that exactly the right ratio of red and white blood corpuscles was racing thru his veins. He was such an overwhelming exponent of good health that I felt a mad desire to chin myself on the privy door and show off in some other equally revolting manner. "You must be Phyllis, late of the Girl Scouts," he said, and I thought I detected a bit of admiration in his voice. I surmised that my uncle had told him of my misfortune, so I said, "Yes, and what's your name?" "Norman Smith," he said. I thought to myself, you might have known it. My aunt and uncle's name was Brown, the Jones were their neighbors on the right and then to have Smiths on the left really simplified matters.

During this exhilarating conversation, I had noticed three children, two boys, and a girl battling with each other down on the dock. A tired looking gray-haired woman was banging pots and pans around the camp kitchen in a listless sort of way. She finally emerged on the back porch, and called "Norma." She called twice, and in man fashion, he ignored her. It was very embarrassing for me, so I said finally, "Your wife is calling you." I had observed Norm's gray hair, the woman's gray air and the three children, so naturally I concluded it was the old story of love, courtship, marriage, kids. He looked up and said, "That's not my wife, it's my Mother."

I don't know why the knowledge of this man having a mother startled me so. I rather imagined that Charles Atlas and Bernard McFadden had collaborated and conjured him up at the most recent physical culture convention; so it didn't occur to me then to wonder about his wife. I decided to go back to my uncle's, and ask questions about the Smiths, then call again some other day. As I was taking my leave, Norm asked me if I would like to go to the movies at the Pier that night. I said that I would ask my uncle's permission and he went on to say that he always went to the early show, as it was the sleep you got before twelve that counted. We went to the show and driving down the bumpy road to our cabin that night, Norm remarked casually that I better marry him and go home with him nights, as our road was knocking hell out of his car. This romantic proposal was followed by an invitation to take part in the family health routine for the rest of the summer. That was the first inkling I had that Norm liked me and from then on our courtship was strictly one of survival of the fittest. I was called upon to arrive at the Smith camp at the ungodly hour of seven each morning.

As soon as I arrived we would don boxing gloves and bat the daylights out of each other for a full half hour. Norm would take on all four of us; Bob, Norma, Wade and me and if he thought one of us was getting off too easy, he would administer his specialty, a kidney punch. I confided in my uncle after the first week that I fully expected to end up in the Smithsonian (no pun intended) Institute with a large sign around my neck saying, "Look, no kidneys."

The next half hour was devoted to calisthenics and then came breakfast. I should explain that all meals were eaten outside at a large picnic table, rain or shine. For breakfast we each had a Kraft cheese glass full of orange juice with which we washed down with cod liver oil. We lingered at the table until each of us had polished off a full quart of milk accompanied by a variety of cold cereals. After a short rest period, in which we were allowed bathroom privileges, we took off for the beach.

The purpose of the daily trip to the beach was twofold. We could walk the length of the beach twice to tone up our leg muscles and then plunge into the surf and play seal for a good hour. The swim, and I use the word with reservation, was considered a complete flop if we didn't keep the two life guards on pins and needles the whole time we were in the ocean. We kids would be floundering around in water over our heads and then Norm would stand waist high and rest while we battled with the elements. When we became nicely waterlogged, the signal to make for shore was given by the Simon Legree of the Atlantic coast and we couldn't get there soon enough. The use of towels to dry one's body was frowned upon by Norm, so we stood there and let the ocean breeze whip our salt incrusted bodies dry. One day, I started to sit down and Norma looked very alarmed and said, "Don't do that. Dad doesn't like us to get sand in our seats," so from then on I stood and consoled myself by thinking that Lot's wife didn't have a thing on me. When completely dry, we would run, not walk, to the pavilion for lunch. Norm couldn't pass up the opportunity of incorporating a two hundred yard dash in the day's routine, and as soon as we reached the verandah, the lifeguards would climb down from their tower, heave a sigh of relief and lunch in peace.

Promptly at two we would leave the beach. Norm explained that the ultra-violet rays were at their best between ten and two, so after bleeding the sun dry each day, we would seek diversion at the Rhode Island College tennis courts. My first day on the court proved to Norm that I wasn't even remotely related to the Falkenburg family, but he was ever hopeful.

Late one afternoon, after a particularly harrowing day, Norm drove into the small cemetery in which his wife and the children's Mother was buried. To me it seemed like a very normal, natural sort of thing. In fact, as we drove away, I thought to myself that next year at the same time they might be paying their respects to me also. I didn't see how I could keep up to the Smiths and live to tell about it.

After two weeks of exercise with Smith, Inc. I had lost ten pounds and developed large lavender shadows where my eyes used to be; and it was then that Norm decided our posture left much to be desired. He came home from marketing one day, lined us up by the front porch and looked our posture over. Bob and I tried our best, but evidently it wasn't good enough; for Norm remarked that we all looked as though we had been fathered by "The Hunchback of Notre Dame." He went on to say that he was planning to take us all on a deep sea fishing trip, but wouldn't consider it unless our posture improved within the next few days.

The remedy for round shoulders was a very simple matter. All you needed to do was to stand up as tall as you could and then imagine that you were being suspended from the top of your dome by a rope, sort of like a marionette. The idea appealed to Norma and Wade, but Bob and I weren't as easily convinced. We two were so tired that we wished someone would sink a rope in our skulls and drag us around.

That evening when I went tripping into my uncle's campsite practicing the suspension theory, he looked up from his dinner and asked, "What the heck is the matter with you?" I explained that I was being motivated by a rope attached to the sky and that my feet were barely touching the ground. He sighed deeply and said, "Thank God your mother will be home next week and put an end to all this nonsense."

THREE ACRES
And Six Dependents

Three days later, Norm dropped his paternity suit against "The Hunchback of Notre Dame" and announced that we could go with the faculty of Rhode Island State College on their annual fishing trip. We drove down to the quaint little fishing village of Galilee, and from the number of times we heard "Jesus " mentioned by the old salt who owned the boat, we knew we were in the right town. As we boarded the boat, I over heard one faculty wife say to another, "There's that poor Norman Smith; wife died last summer and left him with all those kids." I was sixteen at the time and definitely out of my class with all the intelligentsia; but nevertheless resented being classed with "all those kids." Little did I realize how convenient it was going to be when the conversation got around to Einstein, and his theory of relativity. It was so easy just to be seen and not heard.

Norm pointed out to us his various instructors, B.S., M.S., D.D.L. and we tried to act interested, and after a while I nudged Bob and said to Norm, "Who's the old S.O.B. with the handle bar mustache?" That ended the discussion, but the S.O.B. kept hanging around and upon being introduced launched into a lengthy conversation concerning sea sickness and how it was purely mental. We all had been warned by Norm earlier that day that he would not tolerate anybody being sick; so we all more or less agreed with the old boy.

I still felt a bit out of place, but three hours later a degree meant nothing. Most of the faculty had taken on a greenish cast and no one realized it was time to eat. That is no one except the Smith outfit. It was noon, and we were famished; so Norm brought out the lunch. Bob had warned me that his father's lunches left much to be desired, and seeing was believing. The sandwiches were colossal. Whole tomatoes had been forced between slices of bread and store cheese was living in sin with soggy saltines. However, the piece de resistance of the lunch proved to be the drink. This concoction was referred to lovingly by Norm and the kids as punch. After swallowing some, I was dubious. It tasted like the Providence River to me and later on one of Norm's college friends named it "belly wash" and the name stuck. It was weeks before I learned the secret formula. It was made with prepared pudding, water, and a liberal amount of sugar.

After lunch, we sat out on the bowsprit, and I could feel Norm's warm breath on my neck and forgot all about the gruesome food, the sick intellectuals, and the fact that not one of us had caught any fish, My emotions were definitely at war with each other and I kept wondering if this was love.

Mother Meets Norm

When we returned to camp that afternoon, after stopping at the Galilee fish market to buy swordfish for dinner, Grandma Smith met us with the good news that my Mother had arrived that day and was most anxious to behold her one and only daughter. I immediately forgot foot balance, proper breathing technique, dome suspension, but promptly broke the summer's record for the two-hundred yard dash. Upon nearing my uncle's cabin, I slowed down to a walk so I could creep up and take a peek at my mother. One of her friends had taken the same cruise to Greenland the previous summer and had returned bedecked in walrus tooth jewelry and I was fearful that Mother might have succumbed to the charm of the Eskimo costume jewelry. Fortunately she hadn't, so I burst into the family circle and to this day I've never forgotten the look of amazement on my mother's face. Her brown eyes traveled over my gaunt frame, she touched the purple rings beneath my eyes and then shook her head in despair. "Your uncle has been telling me about the man next door," she said, "and what have you to say about yourself, young lady?" I thought a minute and realized it would do no good to flex my muscles, offer to box with my uncle, or submit to a lung X-ray to prove how superbly I could breathe, so I stood there like a dope and stammered, "Mother, you'll like him, he's so, so healthy." I knew it was the wrong approach when Mother snapped, "Probably so, but what about you?"

Just then the three Smith kids arrived on the scene and stood by the door digging their bare feet in the dirt, and not saying a word. Mother glanced up and asked, "Who are the refugees?" My kind uncle broke the news as gently as he could that the three children belonged to the man we had been discussing. Bob, being the oldest and boldest, said, "Here", and thrust a crumpled note into my nervous hand and then all

41

three took another long, sorrowful look before scampering away. The note was an invitation to dine with the Smiths that night as Norm and Grandma were anxious to see my Mother.

We found Norm in the same position I had first seen him in; but since I had shared with him all the fire starting tips, "Big Chief" and Pocahontas had so lovingly bestowed upon me, he was doing a very convincing job.

We marched up to him and I said, "Norm, this is Mother," and he won her over right away with his shy grin and big, sad eyes.

After dinner we sat around and talked and with each mention of higher education, Mother became more intrigued with Smith. When she found out from Grandma that Norm had his Master's Degree, I could see that she was mentally ordering a Lane cedar chest and was resigning herself to my early marriage. We were getting along famously until

Mother casually mentioned in the conversation something about the winter I had spent at Hoxie. This unassuming five letter word means nothing to the residents of the Back Mountain region, but the mere mention of the word strikes terror in the hearts of residents of the small state of Rhode Island. Hoxie and tuberculosis were practically synonymous; one could not exist without the other. At the word Hoxie,

Norm turned pale and the swordfish backed up into his nose and he whispered, "No, no" in an unbelievable manner. It was cruel and Mother let him enjoy that high moment of agony before telling him that I was there simply because my brother Ken had a spot on one lung, and as she and Dad were to go abroad that winter, they figured I might as well be at the sanitarium for tubercular children as in a school somewhere.

Right now, I would like to say that winter was the worst one I ever lived through. The Scout camp was a country club in comparison to Hoxie. In the first place, everyone resented me because I had perfect lungs and all my ribs and planned to hang onto them indefinitely. Clothes were considered an unnecessary evil so we were forced to play out in the snow with heavy boots, mittens, shorts and earmuff hats, and that's all, brother. Legs and arms and chests were at old man winter's disposal and he really took advantage of us. I hated this form of organized play and soon caught on to a little scheme whereby I eliminated the morning frolic in the snow. One day I noticed some of the inmates on an enclosed porch, in the same form of undress of course, but nevertheless sitting and gamboling around in the great outdoors. Before long I found out they were the bed wetters and were made to sit out with their own mattress until old Sol dried them out. Every morning after that when reveille sounded, I would dash to the washroom, fill a paper cup with water, run back and douse my bed liberally. From then on I was a regular member of the mattress brigade and sat on the porch mornings and took no end of delight in thumbing my nose at my brother whenever he came in view.

When Mother and Dad returned from their travels, I was removed from Hoxie with the promise that they would replace my soggy mattress with a new Beauty rest. Poor Ken had to stay there and on the day of my departure I gave him the information he craved most, and that was how to be a morning porch sitter. My Dad listened in great amusement and said, "Maybe I should order two Beauty rests."

On our way home that night, I walked with Mother and whispered, "Mother, what do you think of him?" She squeezed my hand and replied, "Very, very healthy.

THE HONEYMOON

The summer passed all too quickly and Norm returned to his teaching job in Pennsylvania and I returned to Providence to attend school. We saw each other at Christmas time then not until summer. At first we were like strangers, but one picnic took care of that. We had taken Norm's three kids along as well as Bob's best friend, Erving. After we finished our lunch, Norm managed to send the gullible two, Norma and Wade, off in search of violets; but Bob and Erving stayed with us. Erving finally became alarmed at being glared at by Norm and backed off a few feet and pretended to look for a four leaf clover. Bob remained by my side, so Norm gave up and reached over and stuck two big fingers in Bob's eyes and proceeded to kiss me for the first time. A few seconds later, we looked up to see four pair of eyes staring at us in utter fascination. The violet pickers had returned, Erving hadn't found any four leaf clovers and was standing there wearing that "wait until I go home and tell my Mother" expression. Bob was jumping up and down and howling and cussing at having his eyes pushed into his skull. Norm blushed and asked me how I liked being kissed. Like most men he considered his technique above reproach, so who was I to say it felt like being smothered to death by a wet towel in a Turkish bath with all the attendants looking on. Instead I said, "I bet you're the type that likes to swallow goldfish too," and all notions of romance fled.

Not too long after that picnic word got around that I was setting my cap for Norm and he confided in some close friends that I could run faster than he could anyway.

June, 1937 found us married, but not without a heated argument, as to whether young Wade should accompany us on our wedding trip or not. Norm couldn't understand why I didn't want the child along, and Wade's persistent argument was that he had never been on a honeymoon

44

before. No one seemed to realize or care that I hadn't either; but I succeeded in bribing Wade by promising to take him along on my next honeymoon.

Norm chose the twenty-second of June for our wedding day as the Red Sox would be in St. Louis and he had our itinerary planned so that we wouldn't miss any of the Red Sox home games in Boston. I used to feel sorry for the poor souls that went to Niagara Falls, but after spending two weeks in Fen Way Park, I thought more of Niagara Falls as a newlywed's

Mecca. I felt better acquainted with Jimmy Fox, Lefty Grove and Joe Cronin at the end of two weeks than I did with my own husband. The following week the Red Sox left for Detroit and there was no alternative except to go back to camp and face life.

We stopped in Providence to see Mother and pick the three children up and Norm was in for a rare treat. There was a strange man sitting in Mother's living room and Norm asked me, "Who's the stranger?" and when I looked I gave a squeal of recognition and exclaimed, "That's my Dad." I hadn't seen Mr. Micawber (as we fondly and otherwise called him) for almost two years and it was a touching reunion. Mr. Micawber was possessed with the rare talent of going out for a walk and not returning for a year or two and when he did, he always had the air of a man who had just been out to get the Sunday papers. Mother came in and greeted us and said to me, "I just loved the postcard from Norm."

"What card?" I asked and she showed it to me. It was a garish picture of the interior of Fen Way Park and Norm's greeting was brief and to the point. It read, "No hits, no runs, no errors."

Mother asked Mr. Micawber how long he planned to be in Providence and he said a week or ten days, so Mother dashed to the phone and called my aunt and uncle. They decided that we would have a big party just to prove to some people that Mother had a husband and I had a father, plus the attraction of a new husband and son-in-law. Fifty people came and saw and departed shaking their heads in disbelief. Mother and Aunt Stella were sticklers for conversation, but with Norm, Mr. Micawber, my Uncle Sam and myself to contend with, they had a rough evening. My father, a handsome brute, was suffering with a toothache, so every few minutes he would leave the receiving line and disappear into the back entry to be comforted by my uncle who would join him there. The three kids were there and once during the evening Wade placed a foot-stool in the center of the living room, sat down, removed his shoes and proceeded to scratch both feet with great vigor. Norma had gotten into the spirit of the thing and was around telling people how "her Mother" did this and how "her Mother" said this and that. Bob visited the punch bowl once too often and had fallen asleep on a chair in the library. After the last of the guests had departed, Mother and Aunt Stella sat on the loveseat and agreed with each other that except for a few minor details, it had been a truly beautiful party. As we started upstairs, Mother said, "Phyllis, be sure to say goodnight to your father; he may not be here in the morning."

The next morning we left Providence and drove down to South County with the three kids and then the full impact of my new responsibilities hit me. All of a sudden it dawned on me that I would have to wash, iron, and cook for four other people. I knew I loved Norm, so I didn't tell him I was praying for lightning to strike me down before it was time to leave for Kingston, Pennsylvania.

Reality Sets In-I'm a Stepmother

Wyoming Valley wasn't too much of a shock to me as I had visited here once before we were married. My first thought upon weaving down the mountain was wondering what charming bank the Chamber of Commerce was buried beneath. The whole atmosphere was one of great dejection and if I felt depressed when I left Rhode Island, the mutilated earth surrounding Wilkes-Barre did nothing to gladden my heart.

At this time, Norm was renting one half of a weather beaten old farmhouse in Huntsville. I had visited there once and I found it quite comfortable, but far from being my dream house. I knew it wasn't my dream house when I went to rearrange the furniture and found that Norm and his interior decorator, a callow youth called Dusty, had prepared and painted around the larger pieces of furniture instead of moving them into the center of the room. After two weeks, I decided that the old coal stove had no intention of cooperating with me. I had a washing machine, but no set tubs and besides, it got mighty lonesome out there with Norm and the kids away all day long. One night we made doughnuts and there wasn't enough room in the kitchen for the blasted things once we fried them. To me that was the last straw and I cried and said I wouldn't live in a house that didn't have a kitchen large enough to cool doughnuts in.

The next day I found a house right by a grocery store and across the street from a drug store. Planning menus was very different for me, and I would invariably forget something essential to the meal. For the first two months there in Shavertown, the kids would practically knock each other down on the way to and from the store during the dinner hour. The drug store was a popular spot and provided us with desserts until I learned how to bake.

For three whole months I lived in a fool's paradise. I knew no one and the census taker was my fifth caller. He was a wheezy little man who took his job very seriously. He asked me all kinds of questions as to how many children we had, etc., and I answered honestly. When he asked me my age, I said eighteen, and he wrote that down very carefully and after more questions departed. About dinner time a knock came at the front door and it was the census taker back. Norm went to the door and was confronted by "Wheezy" whose face was florid and whose voice sounded like someone walked on spilled sugar. "Does your wife know it's a federal offense to lie about her age?" asked Wheezy. It seems that Wheezy had gone home and was looking over his day's work and came across an eighteen-year-old mother with three kids ranging from six to ten and he was much annoyed. Norm was very helpful and leaned over and whispered to Wheezy that we were married when I was ten and no one but we three and the entire U.S. Government knew about it. So Wheezy departed, horrified, but satisfied.

My second caller was a personable woman who asked me if I would like to join a bridge club she and some friends were forming. I accepted in a moment of weakness and could hardly wait for Norm to come home so I could tell him about it. When I told him, he looked at me and asked the sixty-four dollar question, "Do you know how to play bridge?" "No," I replied, "and what are we going to do about it. I can't back out now." Norm thought and then said there were only three things to remember when playing bridge. Never put an ace on the bottom of the deck, spit on the cards and say seven come eleven, and with this helpful information, I sallied forth to play bridge the following week. What happened to me that day shouldn't have happened to a dog, but fortunately the girls were busy changing from auction to contract so I gathered some information and kept very quiet. I am convinced that after I left, the girls stayed on to find out where Laverne had dug me up.

I really got to know the kids that winter and soon discovered that Norma loved anything dramatic. I have no doubt that I was a regular old witch when she got through describing me to her playmates. One day she went to a birthday party at a friend's without mentioning it to me. I canvassed the neighborhood about five-thirty and found out from another friend's mother where Norma was. When Norm arrived home I took the car and called for Norma. The birthday girl's mother met me at the door with a sad puss and whispered pleadingly, "Please don't beat her." I was nonplussed for a moment, but came to my wits and replied that I wasn't planning to, but it was a good idea. I was highly indignant upon arriving home and told Norm and asked him what I should do and he said, "Beat her" and we both laughed and thought it a good joke.

However, then and there I decided that being a stepmother is a thankless job. If the kids turn out all right, it's because their own mother was such a fine woman, but if they turn out to be hellions, it's because you are such a stinker.

THE HOPELESS CHEST

I think it was in Shavertown that I first became furniture conscious and ever since, Norm has been kept more or less unconscious paying the bills as I have run the gamut from eighteenth century mahogany to my present love, country pine, maple and cherry. I found a very congenial friend for this time consuming hobby and we helped keep Stoher and Fister in Scranton going financially for a couple of years. Our weekly jaunts to Scranton annoyed our husbands no end, not to mention Mr. Quinn – the long-suffering clerk who had learned not to depend on us for his weekly bonus. Norm soon learned that when I came downstairs with my hat on, a trip to Scranton was the inevitable. He didn't pay too much attention until a rather big bill arrived and did I laugh when he made the check out to "Thorn and Thistle" instead of "Stoher and Fister". Norm always has been that conveniently half deaf type who hears everything you don't want heard and nothing you want heard, so I never let on that there was anything wrong with the name "Thorn and Thistle." Mr. Quinn, the salesman the store had assigned to us for our weekly forays, was completely lacking in humor and wasted no time in calling my attention to the error. In fact, he produced the check and waved it in front of our noses in a very injure manner. Margie looked it over and said, "Mr. Quinn, any dope can tell that that means Stoher and Fister," and Mr. Quinn's feelings for us took a quick lurch into reverse.

One day we arrived in Scranton later than usual and as fate would have it, Mr. Quinn was out to lunch. When we two crashed through the swinging doors in our usual quiet and unobtrusive manner, the whole place changed tempo and we swore later that they must have seen us coming. Women clerks started dusting in a fury, gentlemen clerks studied intricate turnings on the legs of sofas and no one let on that two customers had arrived. Undaunted, we took the elevator up to our favorite haunt, the Whitney maple house, and made ourselves at home. The moment Mr. Quinn came in for lunch, he was shoved bodily into the closet elevator in the living room of the maple house where we were relaxing on wing chairs by the fake fireplace. We had been sitting there so long that Margie had become very fond of her chair and almost had decided to buy it; not only for a conversation piece, but to establish herself as a potential customer of Stoher and Fister. Margie caught sight of Mr. Quinn as he emerged from the elevator and started toward the maple house at a brisk trot. He slowed down as he approached us and Margie said to me in an undertone, "Watch this reaction." She spoke out like a woman who had bought many chairs, on many occasions in many different places. "Mr. Quinn, I'll take this chair." With that, Mr. Quinn sank onto the sofa and we all looked at each other in an unbelieving manner. Margie was showing great courage, as her husband couldn't see the necessity of two people having more than two chairs and this would make chair number three. All I could do was to mutter, "Wait until Sparks hears about this." I was interested in a chair, too, but we decided to wait until the following week to buy it, as we didn't want to spoil Mr. Quinn. We took the elevator down and sailed by the clerks who were no longer dusting and waved a fond goodbye to Mr. Quinn and promised in loud tones to return the following week.

Meanwhile, Norm had caught some of our enthusiasm and hied himself down to a furniture store and bought me the most hideous hope chest I ever hope to see. The day it arrived, I couldn't believe my eyes, and I tried to convince the truck driver that he had made a mistake, as I didn't think Norm capable of such horrible taste. It was a monstrosity complete with cedar lining, many different little compartments, an electric clock, and Lord knows what else. The kids were bug-eyed when they came home from school and I heard Wade tell Norma that it really was a fancy coffin with lots of carvings.

As I prepared dinner that night, I was pondering on how I could tell Norm in a kind way that I couldn't live in the same house with that relic from a screwball's renaissance. He came home all smiles and asked me how I liked it. I said, "Fine, but they forgot the glasses and ice bucket." He looked very hurt and said, "It's a hope chest, not a portable bar," and

I said, "Oh". That night I came down with measles, so I had Dr. Davis tell Norm that I was allergic to hope chests as well as to germs.

Two weeks later, the truck driver called for the chest and instead of a refund, which the company would not hear of, we took it out in trade. We came home with two occasional chairs, a bookcase, a coffee table, a card table and an end table, almost. The salesman was pointing out the virtues of this particular end table as Norm said he would like a good end table made of either cast iron or cement preferably. The forceful person we were transacting our business with went on to say this table was strong enough that you could stand on it and the moment his back was turned, Norm stood on it. A loud splintering noise reverberated through the furniture lover's paradise and the unsuspecting salesman moaned, "mine cave-in" and then caught sight of one Norman Smith. I have always worshipped Norm's great presence of mind and upon this occasion, he didn't let me down. He said, pointing, "We'll take this, and this, and this, and when he came to what had once been a table he said, "I don't think we'll take that" and we backed out as gracefully as we could.

That night, I thanked Norm for his good nature about not keeping the hope chest and he said, philosophically, "While there's life, there's no hope chest" and the first crisis in our married life was a thing of the past.

Shopping With Norm

I have a sneaking suspicion that Norm will never fall heir to the title of "Favorite Customer of the Year" if our local department stores were given to sponsoring such contests. He took me over to Wilkes-Barre one day that first fall and showed me around. We parked behind the Boston Store and went in through the rear entrance. Norm stopped to talk to two gentlemen and I went blithely on my way thinking all the time that Norm was at my side. A few seconds later I realized I was carrying on a spirited conversation with myself so I stopped and looked around for Norm.

One of the endearing things about Norm is that he is always so easy to find in a crowd. He was way at the back of the store and motioned with great vigor for me to go on and do my shopping and then return to where he was standing. I did and before too long discovered that I was being followed. A rather young man was hot on my trail and stopped at every counter I stopped at. I didn't mind too much until I stopped at the underwear counter and he halted, too. I was by then annoyed and it was hard for me to decide if I wanted small, medium or large in the briefs I had decided to buy with this young man watching every move I made. I thought maybe the store provided this obnoxious type of guardian angel service until I noticed other women going about their shopping completely unmolested.

I knew the store had more than one floor, but I decided to tour the rest some other day when the leech wasn't around. I pranced out the rear door after giving Norm the signal to join me and he came out grinning from ear to ear. "They really have an efficient detective system in that store," he volunteered and I stopped dead in my tracks and said, "What did you say?" He repeated that the store's detective system was very efficient and I asked, "How do you know?" He replied, "Did you notice that young man who followed you around?" I was tempted to reply, "No, what man?" but was so burned up I said, "Notice him, all I have to say is that it's a darn good thing I didn't have to go to the rest room". Norm then told me the two men he had stopped to talk to were Alec Dick and Frank Burnside and that he had pointed me out to them as a notorious shoplifter just to see what would happen. Frank couldn't locate a detective so took the job upon himself and thought it a wonderful joke when Norm told them later that I was his new wife. I didn't think it too humorous at the time, but now when I see the Burnsides we are apt to reminisce about my introduction to the Boston Store, and all enjoy a hearty laugh.

When my first bill came from the Boston Store, Norm scanned it briefly and sent a check covering both the credit and debit column. The following month we had a nice sum in the credit column, but Norm sent another check covering everything on the bill. You think it impossible on a school teacher's salary, but nevertheless it happened. This went on for several months until Norm received a sizable check from the Boston Store and a letter begging him to stop overpaying the bill. It seems that the bookkeeper was becoming glassy-eyed and jittery trying to balance our account.

I distinctly remember a choice bit of correspondence Norm had with Isaac Long. We had been in Rhode Island for the three summer months, so I naturally had not charged anything at Isaac Long's. We found their usual courteous form letter in our mail inquiring as to whether there was any particular reason why I had not availed myself of the opportunity of using their charge account. Norm took it upon himself to answer their letter and wrote across the bottom of the page, "Don't worry, my wife had been out of town, but she's back; and now it's my turn to worry." To my knowledge it's the only time in the history of Isaac Long's that a customer ordained to answer one of those letters; and Isaac's not to be outdone, answered Norm's letter; but on a clean piece of paper. They thanked Norm for his amusing reply and closed in the usual manner of wishing to be of service to us, etc. This time he wrote across the bottom of their letter, "If you really want to be of service to me, you'll close my wife's charge account," and that ended that.

I realize that none of Norm's letters will ever be published in an anthology of the world's great letters, but should some wit publish an edition of the world's zaniest letters, Norm might come into his own. The following would be my contribution from Norm to humanity. In a house Norm once lived in, long before I knew him, the roof developed a very annoying leak. This leak might have gone unnoticed for years by Norm except for the fact that it was directly over his bed. Instead of telling the landlady of the trouble, he got out his trusty portable and typed the following lengthy message. "The roof leaks." The landlady, being an equally gregarious soul wrote back, "You must be mistaken." Norm wrote back, I haven's wet my bed in years. It must be the roof." The generous landlady had one shingle nailed on the roof directly over Norm's bed and the problem was solved. He has always pointed out that incident to me as a good example of getting things done the painless way and I don't know but what he was right.

Product Demo Dinners

The winter flew by and to say my social life was gay would be a deliberate lie. Besides the bridge club I am willing to wager, I attended every cooking utensil dinner held; plus two very enlightening brush demonstrations. Of the two, I feel the cooking utensil dinners will live on in my memory and as I near as I know, they are not extinct. Some enterprising salesman would find out about a woman whose pots and pans were in a deplorable condition; or else clip the picture of a new bride from the paper; and to use a trite phrase, their goose was cooked.

The salesman would call on the lady of his choice and give her a super special sales talk and at the same time would be eyeing with obvious nausea the beat-up saucepan reposing on the stove. If you agreed to have a demonstration, you would be given some small token in memory of the occasion. One of my friends was presented with an omelet pan, so naturally eggs became the major item on her budget. Her husband finally started to raise chickens to make possible the frequent use of the gift. I have always been thankful that Norm fell for the twelve cup drip coffee pot; so while my friend crawls in and out of an incubator, I remain indoors and drink coffee.

Assuming that the woman victim and her family alone were not enough to justify this great interest in the future, the hostess was asked to invite a few friends in for dinner. To me it was always an easy group to be with as we all had so much in common; loose handles, warped bottoms and makeshift double boilers. All conversation centered around food, and what it was prepared in. Once the guests all arrived, the entertainment started. The salesman had a short, little thirty minute talk scheduled which gave the dinner ample time in which to wither and decay. All speeches were in the same vein and you always received the impression that you had been poisoning your family for years by not using his specific brand of utensils. I was always tempted to race to the phone to call and inquire if any of the Smiths had been taken by the goulash I left in some innocent looking pan.

After that terrorizing chat, we were asked to partake of the dinner. We were shown at close range how the potatoes had been riced, not mashed in a cumbersome gadget slightly smaller than a washing machine. The only two drawbacks as far as I could see were that it was almost impossible to wash said gadget clean and it would take up the entire cupboard space in the average American kitchen. We were impressed with the fact that no water was used in preparing the meal and I used to wonder how the coffee was conceived. Applesauce was usually on the menu, but had been made earlier in the day and forced through the ricer, which made two legitimate reasons why no normal person could keep house without one.

My last dinner was the one I took Norm to. One girl had the bright idea of letting the husbands in on a demonstration and we concluded later that it hadn't been such a bright ideal after all. Norm and one of his pals we call "Gloves" came close to causing a riot in the hostess's kitchen. They had become bored with the before dinner speech so wandered out to the kitchen to see for themselves what was cooking in what. They proceeded to lift the lids off every pot on the stove making possible the escape of most the precious vitamins we had been hearing about; not to mention the odor of rebellious cabbage; which up to that moment had been a carefully guarded secret. The salesman cut his talk short and gave the hostess a very desperate "let's dish up the dinner" look, then tore out to the kitchen. By that time Norm and "Gloves" were sampling the coffee and volunteered the information that it was as good as Salvation Army coffee any day.

To give credit where credit is due, I will say that both Norm and "Gloves" bought their unhappy wives a ricer and then they suggested that we all go down to the diner for hamburgers.

The brush demonstrations will not be discussed here for the obvious reason that they always remind some one of a joke. Suffice it is to say, there is a brush for every occasion, but not necessarily an occasion for every brush.

Worn Out At A Rest Camp

As soon as school was out in June, we packed three barrels and sent them on by freight to Rhode Island; then collected the three Smith kids and headed for home. We found the cabin pretty much as we had left it and in no time at all, we were back in the old routine. By some fast talking, I talked myself out of the morning boxing bouts, but partook of all the other strenuous activities. We had planned to leave the children with their grandmother and see all of the New England states at our leisure and I might add; between baseball games. Norm announced that we could very nicely manage a trip to Vermont to visit the Sparks and I was pleased beyond words. Margie and Ray were spending the summer at an exclusive rest camp for alcoholics. I should make it clear that our friends were there on the administrative basis rather than that of the paying guest.

Our visit took place in August, and by then our pals were in fine physical condition and used to the high altitude. We arrived late one afternoon, had dinner with guests, and were advised to get a good night's rest as our host had a full day planned for us. We were making out famously until one of the older male guests spied our golfing equipment. Before we realized what was happening, the lady in charge was assuring us that it would be perfectly all right to take Rob golfing the next day. She took us aside and assured us that he was as good as cured, but hoped we wouldn't influence him in any way. I hastily explained that Norm's strongest drink was a double malted and that Bob could not be safer with his own mother.

We three took off bright and early the next morning and drove to the "Corn Hill Country Club." I noted with horror that it was a full-fledged eighteen hole golf course, and that our new found friend had undoubtedly devoted his whole life to golf and "Four Roses"! Every hole was like mountain climbing, but at every few holes there was a dispenser for ice cold beer or coke. Our friend never let on that there was liquid refreshment nearby and fear kept us away from the dispensers. After thirty-six holes, I staggered over to the car and collapsed, and waited expectantly for the men to join me; but our pal was still fresh as a daisy and Norm, not to be outdone, had agreed to go around again. I don't know yet how Norm convinced him that 54 holes were enough for one day.

When we returned to the so-called rest camp, our hostess announced that we were going to have a picnic supper. I had always loved picnics, but the mere thought of tripping over some more mountains just to eat was revolting. Our destination was reached after a short jaunt of four miles; but the waterfall was pretty. I sat there trying to decide whom I would like to see tossed into the icy water first; our hostess or the Bobby Jones of Alcoholics Anonymous who was roasting hot dogs with the vigor of a man just up from a nap. My eyes kept closing and every time they did I could vision a substantial old four poster beckoning to me, but there was still the walk home. I made it; how I'll never know, and before I could blurt out goodnight, we were informed that a Finnish bath was in order. A bath in any language has always been a thing of necessity rather than joy to me, but Ray and Margie soon talked me into submission. Our host explained the bath to us. It's an old Finnish custom to repair to a small constructed hut, complete with benches and a wall of red hot stone heated by a massive fireplace. The procedure was to undress, seat yourself and make everything right with your Maker, then prepare yourself for the steaming of your life. Your first reaction is that you are going to die, then you wish to heck you would, anything to prevent being cooked alive in that man-made Dante's inferno. At first we sat there making idle stabs at conversation, but that soon became too much of an effort. We had been told that this was a painless way to lose weight and of course that appealed to me, but it was horrible to sit there and feel all your sex appeal melting away and not be able to do anything about it. As soon as the steam would start to die down, Ray with maddening German precision, would dash another bucket of water onto the red hot stones. Norm muttered that you could never trust a Henie anyway and Ray definitely had the upper hand. Our only hope was that we would eventually run out of water. I came to later and heard Ray announce that he was about to open the door and let us escape. Right by the door was an ice cold pool of water into which we were to leap; the theory being that shock revived you. I fell into this torture hole and beyond that I have no memory. I guess Norm hauled me out and got me into bed. We didn't wake up until four o'clock the next afternoon. Norm and I looked at each other and I said, "Why, we didn't die, did we?" and he replied, "No, but we might as well be dead as the way we are." Norm then gave birth to a marvelous thought which boiled down to leaving the rest camp, but quick before Ray had another brainstorm. We found Ray and Margie, were shadows of their former selves, said goodbye and headed for civilization which to us meant Boston and the Red Sox

Foul Play

During our courtship, I had several inklings as to Norm's complete inability to do anything really creative with a hammer. I recall once at his summer camp, he was fixing the lock on the front door and the next time I went over they had a new front door. One day, he fashioned a ladder out of two slender young saplings and an orange crate as he wanted to get up on the roof and peer down the drainpipe. He got upon the roof all right, but coming down the saplings parted ways and what had shortly before been a ladder was no more. He landed on the ground with a sickening thud and Grandma and I acted as though he had made a perfectly graceful descent from the roof.

Another time he decided to repair the old dock, which I had been damaged by ice during the winter. To make the necessary repairs, he had to stand in about two feet of water. My brother wandered down in all innocence one day to see how the job was progressing and was surprised to see the finished end at a forty-five degree angle. He opened his youthfully large mouth and before he could say a word, Norm said, "You fat-head, it's supposed to be like that." Ken wasn't exactly crushed, but he did say to me, "I just hope you get married and have a lot of little carpenters lousing up the joint," and stomped off. A lot of Norm's relatives visited his mother at camp and Grandma and I were fearful that some unsuspecting soul would venture down on the dock and break a leg. One day while Norm was at summer school, we painted a sign which read, "Keep Off. Unsafe", and nailed it on a conspicuous place on the dock. Norm never let on that is was there, but spent the remainder of his vacation on the far end of the dock trying to prove how wrong the sign was.

The furthest back Grandma and I have been able to trace Norm's love for a hammer is to grammar school days when every boy took a year or two of woodworking. We are both sure his eyes gleamed with pleasure when he contemplated using a hammer and making useful articles out of wood. When the teacher (God rest his soul) announced that a tie rack would be their first project, Norm was beside himself with joy. By Friday of that first week all the boys had simple, but neatly made tie racks to take home. That is all the boys except Norm. That afternoon, the teacher spoke kindly, but firmly, "Hey, you." Those words meant nothing to the John Goddard of the Lexington Grammar School until the teacher repeated, "Hey, you behind the woodpile." Norm arose from the debris he created and walked obediently to the teacher's desk. The teacher simply wanted to know what was the matter as Norm had used up half the semester's supply of wood and still had nothing you would accuse of being a tie rack to take home that day. Norm hung his head in shame and said his father wouldn't like it at all as he had bought Norm a new tie to put on the tie rack he was to bring home.

The next project was a birdhouse and Norm showed no initiative whatsoever. The teacher found out why from one of the other boys. It seemed that Grandma Smith always had so darn many cats around that there hadn't been a bird in Smith's backyard since Norm was born. You could hardly blame the boy for not being mad about birdhouses. Right then the teacher hit upon a plan that suited them both. Every day Norm was to sweep the floor and then be allowed to read the daily paper, and both parties benefited by the new agreement.

Norm has his own ideas about repair work, and anything that can't be fixed with adhesive tape or a monkey wrench isn't worth bothering with. If the adhesive tape manufacturers could see some of Norm's uses for their product, a whole new advertising campaign might be born. When we moved from Shavertown to Trucksville, a leg on our bed was broken.

Norm taped it back on, but even the best adhesive tape manufactured isn't intended to support a man weighing a few pounds less than a horse.

The bed promptly let us down, so Norm was forced into using a saw, an implement about which he knew very little. He decided it would be much simpler to saw off the three remaining legs than to fix the broken leg. This psychology was not a debatable subject with me at two o'clock in the morning, so off came the legs. I sat hunched up in a chair and when the mutilation was complete, Norm stood back and surveyed his work of art. "Looks kind of modernistic, doesn't it?" he asked, and I yawned, "Yes." We stepped down into bed and received quite a shock. The remaining pieces of furniture, and it was a bedroom suite in every sense of the word, towered over us and we both lay there in terror expecting the highboy to fall over momentarily and crush us to death. Norm sighed, got up again and sawed the legs off everything. By that time all the kids were awake in our room and Bob was giving the younger ones heck for not hiding the saw in a better place.

Around our present home there are many obvious examples of Norm's handiwork. I am sure we own the most fantastic chicken coop ever devised. The nests are so high up that nothing short of a pigeon would think of dropping an egg in one. The result is that the girls lay their eggs in all sorts of tricky places. You will never catch a Smith at an Easter egg hunt. We have a daily egg hunt around here. How the hens ever get through the labyrinth connecting their coop with their yard, remains a mystery to me. I think the blueprints were buried last summer when Norm cemented his way around the old barn. Norm's latest creation is a ward for sick chickens which was erected one Saturday when the kids and I were out at Ruggles. It is the kind of thing that brought tears to the eyes of our friends the first time they saw it. What touched them most was a series of perches which no able bodied foul could possibly reach let alone a poor girl in the advanced stages of Coccidiosis.

I see by yesterday's mail that we are now subscribing to the "American Poultry Journal." Anything can happen now, and undoubtedly will.

RECONSTRUCTION ERA

Life in Trucksville went on smoothly. The modernistic bedroom suite was eventually replaced by a mahogany bed and highboy. Margie and I read somewhere that whole suites of matching furniture were becoming obsolete and by that time we were thoroughly confused anyway, but still did business spasmodically with our friend, Mr. Quinn at Stoher and Fister's. We read all the books the Hoyt Library and to offer concerning; our favorite being, "How to be Your Own Decorator" by Helen Koues. We both had our problems, but were not too discouraged. We had found out the hard way that decorating on a shoestring was impossible.

After reading some lilting prose about a smart young woman who had converted a bookcase into a china closet, I promptly tried to imitate the effect. No matter what arrangement we arrived at, it always looked just like a bookcase with china in it. One day, Margie was out and I asked her to get me some tea cups. "Dickens or Longfellow?" she inquired and that did it. That night Norm watched with jaundiced eye as I reconverted the china closet back into a bookcase. This piece of furniture ended up at the United Liquidating Company and was bought, I was told, by a young lady who thought she could use it for dishes. Margie and I just looked smug and thought what a long way that young lady had to go.

A lack of funds and a bit of inner research gave birth that winter to what our husbands referred to as the "Reconstruction Era." We suddenly decided that we were devoting too much time to our houses and not enough to ourselves. We promptly joined the "Book of the Month" club and subscribed to "Time" and read feverishly all the best sellers. No one was aware of this great cultural change except ourselves, but we pursued our new life with great vigor. Margie sprang for a new issue of "Vogue" and we realized with horror that our wardrobes were spineless.

Fur hats were big news that winter and we just knew we had to have them. Margie had an old sealskin coat which had been remade a time or two, but still managed to give the impression that it would have been happier on the seal.

I was none too happy owner of a skunk jacket. The kids claimed it smelled whenever it was rained or snowed upon. New fur coats being out of the question, we went to a hat store and picked out black, felt hats to be trimmed with fur to match our coats. Margie's came down over her right eye and when the fur was added, she looked rather like an Airdale trying to focus her right eye through the fur. For me, they selected a cone shaped number, sort of like a clown's hat, which in itself was bad enough, but when a swirl of skunk was added, which ended in a ball of skunk at the very tip, it was awe-inspiring. When I walked it gave the effect of a miniature cyclone blowing up and people took off in the opposite direction. We were a little self-conscious as we made our way back to the parking lot, but when one man stopped dead in his tracks and said, "Now, I've seen everything," we were thoroughly dubious. Margie looked at me and asked, "What do you think Smith?" I replied, "I feel like I have just been skunked out of ten dollars." We finally reached the shelter of the car and I discovered with great joy that I could not wear my hat in the car unless we cut a hole through the roof. Margie sat be me looking very dejected. Our insides felt like paper-mache and we were both wondering how we could tell our long-suffering husbands about our latest mistake.

This little incident took place a few days before the annual Thanksgiving football classic. Fortunately, it snowed and we were forced to stay in the car. My hat reposed on the front seat by us and the kids kept leaning over the front seat to prod at it and make unkind remarks. When the game was over, Norm climbed in the car and caught a glance of the apparition and asked in true Dogwood fashion, "What's that?" I replied it was my new hat and he said kindly, "That's all right, I won't tell anyone."

When we reached home, I modeled the hat for Norm and his face was a study. He kept staring at it, then at me, so I finally ventured,

"What do you think?" and he said, "I think all you need is a white stripe down your back and an atomizer."

Margie had her troubles, too. She went home and peered through the fur at Ray. He took a long look and then whistled and said, "Here boy, here boy," and thus ended the "Reconstruction Era" as far as our own wardrobes were concerned.

THE MAGIC TOP

My greatest regret in leaving Shavertown for Trucksville was in saying goodbye to a dandy gas stove. It was a thing of beauty done up in several shades of grey, complete with an alarm that rang vigorously and kept many a meal from becoming a burnt offering. In Trucksville we were to have a coal range, so I would be unable to use my magic top. Less this sounds juvenile, or even playful, I should hasten to explain the magic top. It was an eighteen inch square made of heavy alloy and would fit over all four burners on a gas range. The heat from one burner would distribute itself beneath the magic top and a whole meal could be cooked on top by using the smallest burner turned way down low; definitely a great fuel saver. This magic top was the brainchild of a man who rented one of my uncle's apartments in Providence. This gentleman was a salesman par excellence and had bled several communities dry before coming to Providence. He arrived in Providence at the height of the depression, but what money was left in that suffering city, soon found its way into his pocket.

Mr. Shores was a great big man who gave the immediate impression of living well. One glance at him told you that he ate well, drank well, and sold well. Any business which would allow a man to purchase and consume roughly a quart of liquor a day was looked upon in great awe by my brother and me. Up until the time Mr. Shores moved in, one lonesome garbage can reposed in the backyard. The following week my uncle was forced into providing a large receptacle for bottles, medicinal and otherwise, mostly otherwise. This second container caused my mother and aunt a great deal of distress. They were both born in Kansas, but unfortunately a few years too late to accompany Carrie Nation on her clean-up campaigns. It was four years before I knew a drinking establishment was called anything but a saloon and that liquor was the refined name for booze. Mother and Aunt Stella waged a cold war with Mr. Shores Whenever he engaged them in conversation, they would step back a foot or two as though the fumes from the rye he had just gargled with were about to overcome them. They made sly remarks about the poor garbage man who could hardly stagger out on to Parade Street anymore without assistance. My brother was to be an end man in a

Minstrel show and told mother he needed some blackened cork. That was golden opportunity for Aunt Stella to say, "Why don't you have Bill Shores save you the corks from all those booze bottles? You could

blacken the whole cast with a week's supply." Ken simply adored Bill Shores, so asked shyly for the corks and Bill laughed his hearty laugh, and if we hadn't been minors, I'm sure he would have asked us to have a shot with him.

Mr. Micawber had stepped out the previous year for North Dakota, and if my memory serves me right, he and the dust storms hit North Dakota at about the same time. His infrequent, dusty letters contained stark accounts of the suffering that befell man and nature alike that unforgettable year that he was there. Six months later, we received a letter postmarked, Rochester, Minnesota and found out that Mr. Micawber had undergone surgery at the Mayo Clinic in the hope of curing a bad case of ulcers brought on, mother claims from the nervous tension of receiving, selling and never holding a winning ticket for the Irish Sweepstakes.

Meanwhile, mother was waiting for the red tape to go through, so she could resume teaching in the Providence Schools. Mr. Shores was busy giving demonstrations of his magic top and the fabulous cooking utensils which went with it, and could be yours if your husband was affiliated in some way with the Chase National Bank. At that time, Mr. Shores was fresh out of assistants and asked mother if she would like to earn somemoney by helping with the demonstrations. Mother was in no position to refuse his offer, so after being reassured that no sales talks were given in saloons, went along on the deal. The minute she started to work, the sales stopped. They fed fifty people in one week and not one sale was consummated. Mother ended up with a magic top, a set of the utensils, and an inferiority complex. MR. Shores paid his rent, heaved his last empty into the garbage can and left Providence to seek greener fields. Mother gave us the outfit for a wedding present, which in turn gives me a malicious thought. I wonder how Bob, soon to be married, would like the magic top for a gift. Knowing Bob as I do, I can just hear him say, "It's nice, but where's the stove to go with it?"

Buying Our First House

The people who owned our house in Trucksville decided to come back there to live, so we began to think about moving. We had no particular place in mind until Naomi Nuss called me one day and said, "Phyllis, I know of a house here in Huntsville for rent." Unlike present times, there was a choice of places, so I was in no great hurry to drive over to Huntsville. One day the next week, I took Norm to work, then drove out to see Naomi and the house. I liked it immediately, as it was an old farmhouse and rather colonial in feeling, which to one raised in New England is almost a necessity. The interior of the place was rather sad and badly in need of fresh paper and paint, but my enthusiasm knew no bounds. I brought Norm over the following Saturday and he liked the place in a mild sort of way. He was thinking of all the things there would be to do to make it livable. I kept saying, "Norm, it has all sorts of possibilities," and he said, "Yes, I know, but you're the type that can see possibilities in an outhouse," but nevertheless, he agreed to move and give it a whirl. The landlord was very agreeable about our renting it, and gave us a price in case we wanted to buy.

At the time we looked at the house, a dear little old lady was living here with her two sons who we shall call Romulus and Remus. We never found out if there was any wolf in them as we never laid eyes on them. Romulus slept days and gave Greyhound busses baths at night. Remus worked days, so we only knew their mother. The first day when Naomi and I looked at the house, the mother had whooping cough so bad she kept sulphur candles burning to give her some relief. I didn't think to mention the fact to Norm, so when I took him over and we were upstairs looking over the floor plan through a bluish sulphur haze, Norm whispered, "Why didn't you tell me they were Hindus?"

The old place had had many interesting tenants before the Smiths moved in. One man had a mania for nails and Norm yanked over three hundred of them out of the kitchen walls prior to having the kitchen papered and painted. A lad by the name of Tommy had written his name on walls throughout the house and when Norm and I had our first son; Norm suggested with a sadistic gleam in his eye, that we name him Tommy.

The most unusual family was the one that moved out during the night. Before leaving, they had done many things to endear themselves to their landlord. During the long, cold winter they removed the interior of the old barn piece by piece to burn in the furnace and had started on the sidingbefore being detected. Tin cans were no problem at all, as they simply opened the laundry window and tossed them into the yard. One day, when it was too cold to walk down and tear off a piece of the barn, the pipes all froze causing all kinds of damage. These were minor items compared to the fact that it never occurred to them to pay any rent. How the landlord ever got rid of them is a mystery to me. Maybe they found a house with a nice big unmolested barn and proceeded to remodel it in their highly original fashion.

In one corner of the kitchen stood a huge black coal stove. The old carpenter who was working for us helped Norm dismantle it and put it out on the back porch. We asked his advice about what to do with it and he said, "Why don't you sell it?" It was a refreshing idea, but Norm allowed that it would be easier to overthrow the Salvation Army single handed, than to sell anybody anything. We inquired around, but found no buyers. Two weeks later, we tried hard to give it away, but couldn't even find anyone to give it to. We finally had to pay a man to haul it away. The man we paid to haul it away sold it for fifteen dollars, which should give one a rough idea of our astounding business ability.

All this took place in May and I busied myself by picking out completely unrelated wallpaper for each and every room. In June we moved in and a week later, left for Rhode Island to spend the summer. We left the house to the painter, who finished his work inside, then gave the exterior three coats of white which still looks about as good as new.

All this work was done at our own expense, and when we came back in the fall it looked so nice, we were petrified that the owner, who lived out of town would see it looking so attractive and decide not to sell after all. Norm sat down immediately and wrote and told him that we would buy at his price and the deal was carried on through the mail. We both consider that the purchase of this house was about the smartest thing we ever did, but neither of us can figure out how we were smart enough to think of it.

NO BOATS

I will never forget how our house looked that first September, pristine white and sitting on the hillside amid a sea of tall grass. I remarked to Norm that it looked like an ad for "Dutch Boy White Lead" and he nodded and replied, "If we only had a bottle of Seven-Up, we could launch it." The children were cavorting about in the hay, so Norm and I went on inside to view the paint and paper. At that stage of my development the sickly pink of the living room walls, and the bilious green I had liked so well for the dining room that we carried it on into the upstairs hall, affected me not at all. The den paper we both liked. It was Sears and Roebuck's version of a hunting scene, but you soon lost track of the hunters. There were more people engaged in more activities on that wallpaper so that instead of a place of rest, which a den should be, it became a place of inspiration. The room was absolutely pregnant with ideas. You could do anything, but relax in our den. One group of people were fishing, a nostalgic little scene which always reminded some people of the time they had gone fishing and actually caught a fish. The golfer pictured in the sand trap banging his way out received no sympathy from anyone but me. Norm claims he likes to play golf with me as it's so restful. He lounges around while I hunt for balls in the rough and go from trap to trap. The boating group featured two lazy swains relaxing in the sun while their lady loves rowed the old flat bottomed boat up and down the Cambridge River.

We referred to that scene as "Strictly Harvard". The picnickers were enjoying themselves on paper despite the fact that there were more kids than food in evidence; a fact I could appreciate wholeheartedly. We named that scene, "Too Many Brats" much to mother's horror, but she had never gone on a picnic with us and was in no position to judge the name.

In Mother's day, a picnic consisted of driving one of those bucking broncos, misnamed cars, but properly termed horseless carriages to Newport. Once there, they tied up the carriage and walked the length of the famous Cliff Walk fully enjoying the beautiful homes owned by the scions of Wall Street. That was back in the days before the middle classes had been incited against those that dwelt in Newport's marble halls, so Mother never knew any great frustration from viewing those palatial residences from the ocean side. In fact, she probably was of the same mind as her daughter, and undoubtedly remarked how she would hate to do the dusting in an eighty room house. Fortunately in this day and age, most houses have seven rooms and with seven days a week, no outside activities, a really eager beaver can break even by dusting one room a day. How times have changed.

Now to get back to the den paper, I can't remember what the horsemen were up to in that truly delightful paper, and it's for sure that I won't rip off any of the present paper to find out. I think the men were playing polo, but Norm says they were looking for a horse to ride. We'll never be able to duplicate that paper, thank goodness.

I couldn't believe that I had selected the paper in Bob and Wade's room. It was some designer's conception of a seagoing craft, all done in murky tones of brown, none of which could even keep afloat in Posten's Pond. With the addition of maple furniture, the room took on an air of utter desolation and to this day, I marvel at the fact that neither Bob nor Wade became manic depressive. Norm's fondest dream, as a father, was to have his sons go to West Point and make a career of the Army. Bob graduated from Annapolis and is now a Marine, while Wade is giving his best to the Coast Guard Academy, and I am inclined to wonder if the wallpaper had anything to do with it. Our friends know how Norm wanted his sons to go to West Point, but now he is more or less smug about the whole thing and when people start to sympathize with him, he just says, "That's all right; we haven't run out of Smiths yet." If anyone sees a wallpaper which includes Eisenhower, "Pistol Packin" Patton, Iwo Jima and the Battle of the Bulge, would you please let Norm know as we are about to repaper that room for the younger Smith brothers and I promised Norm, "No boats!"

KING

He came to us at dusk nine years ago, on bruised and travel-weary feet. Two months ago, he disappeared into the night on old, experienced feet, never to return. He carved a very special niche in all our hearts which has become a shelf for memory to rest upon. Wade named him "King" and from long-nosed, gangling puppyhood, he grew up to fit the name and wore it like a crown upon his head.

He had his faults to be sure; his very worst one being his inability to resist chasing cars. Old noisy cars were his pet peeve and Clint Ide always claimed, if King chased him he would know it was time to buy a new car. To our knowledge Sheppie who lives down the road from us, was King's only enemy. King could be sound asleep in the living room, and if Sheppie went by in the truck with Mr. Prutzman, King would bristle up all over and bark loudly and long. One day Norm and Keith were polishing their shoes out on the back steps. It was summer and Norm had just remarked to Keith that he thought Mr. Prutzman was going to get by the house once without being barked at when King, who had been asleep on the living room floor, came right through the lower half of the screen door, knocked Keith and the shoe polish off the steps, and proceeded to chase Sheppie and the truck up to the corner.

King joined the K-9 Corps and gave his best to his country in that hell known as the South Pacific. Unfortunately, not much of his war record is known to us, but his honorable discharge papers rest in a leather folder next to Norm's in one part of the desk. In fact, Norm loves to tell his friends about the time he was confined to the Nesbitt Hospital with an ulcer attack. The Veteran's Administration was to take care of the bill, but they needed Norm's discharge papers before they could start the red tape rolling. I went hurriedly to the desk one morning and handed Norm's papers to Wade to drop off at Dr. Davis'. Dr. Davis sent the same to the Veterans and was surprised when he received a phone call inquiring whether he was treating a dog at the Nesbitt. He replied that he wouldn't go so far as to say that. Then he realized what had happened. He called Norm in great glee and explained the situation. Norm gave me full credit for what he thought was a good gag. That evening when I went to see him, he had a large red heart pinned on his nightshirt and he barked when I stuck my head in the door. Norm has been back in the hospital twice since, we can't figure out why he always takes his own credentials down with him. He claims that Veteran's Administration has a whole file on a dog named King who was treated at Nesbitt for ulcers.

Wade and Keith, both sentimentalists at heart, called King "Baby" and miss him most of all. When Keith was a toddler, he fell into the spring and King calmly dragged him out by his straps and laid him at Norm's feet, a muddy, dripping mass of manhood in formation. Those are the things you never can forget.

"Black Beauty", Gross's cocker spaniel, was King's special love and she was devoted to him. Two years ago she died trying to give birth to King's puppies and no other dog ever replaced her in King's affections. For months after, he would go over there and look all around for her and with pleading eyes seeking some explanation from Helen as to Beauty's whereabouts.

Last summer King was run over by a large truck and made it to the old barn before collapsing. We called Dr. Flack and Norm picked King up and put him in the station wagon and we raced over to the Animal Hospital with him. Dr. Flack was very kind and understanding and requested that we leave King there. He had a broken pelvis and internal injuries. Two weeks later Norm brought King home to die, but he staged a

remarkable comeback with the love and care bestowed upon him by all the family. Dr. Flack would stop in about every day to see him and was amazed at his recovery. By fall King was car-chasing again and protesting loudly when Sheppie went by in the truck.

King meant many things to many people. To us he was an honored member of the family. To our friends he was a friend, a welcome addition to any gathering. Our hearts yearn for him, first, last and always, a King among four-footed folk.

Dealing with Door to Door Peddlers

We miss King in another respect these lush spring days. King would never allow salesmen in the yard and we have seen many park a car out front, take a look at King and climb back in their cars and drive away. Norm and I are both highly susceptible to salesmen and are apt to buy any old useless gadget following a good sales talk. Way back in the days before King is when the two mad Armenians sold us some very gruesome Oriental rugs. Word must have reached them that we were gliding aimlessly about the house on cracked congoleum, blissfully unaware of what Orientals could to for our standard of living. Neither Margie nor I had made a study of rugs, but I had read somewhere to beware of rugs with a stiff backing as that denoted a great amount of sizing and in time would deteriorate leaving nothing but a memory of the rug it used to be. I was more than impressed when the two dusky demonstrators walked in with a nine by twelve Oriental done up in a small package, plus several smaller packages, which later proved to be chips off the same warp. In ten minutes the rugs were reposing on the living room floor and I asked Norm what he thought and he said, "It looks like the lobby of the Kingston theatre," but he nevertheless was interested. Meanwhile, both men had their hats pulled down over their eyes and were glancing furtively about and pacing up and down the room. They seemed to be in a great hurry to leave, so pulled their piece de resistance which consisted of lighting matches and throwing them on the rugs which fortunately had been fire-proofed. Norm will buy anything that is fireproof, so after that startling display he located his checkbook and said, "Sold."

Several nights later, some friends called and Norm got some kitchen matches and lighted several and threw them with reckless abandon around the room. Much to his horror they lay smoldering on the rug, so we all jumped up and stepped on them. Norm was crushed and we told our guests what had happened the night the rugs became ours. The man, quiet, but smart, told Norm were the victims of a magnificent hoax. In the first place, the rugs were of Chinese origin and weren't even remotely related to the great Karastan family and in the second place, they weren't fireproof. It was all in the way the men threw the matches. They were out long before they ever hit the rug. The next morning's inspection revealed many little burned places, so we kept the rugs, but never ever lit a match in the same room with them.

Once we purchased the rugs, we were an easy mark for a "beats as it sweeps as it cleans" expert, so every day some poor Chinaman's work was taken up into the hungry Hoover bag. The first week that Norm left to report for duty in Maryland, he cautioned me not to make any big purchases until we decided what we were going to do with the house and kids while he was Special Servicing for Uncle Sam. Norm, it seems to me, was about the first man to report for duty for WWII, and about the last to be discharged. Anyway, his orders came in March and he left the following week for Fort Meade. Just as he drove away, Wade reported that there was a man at the front door to see me. I was in no condition to argue about anything at that point, so in no time at all, repulsive had thrown dirt all over the rugs and was showing why his cleaner was the only one to keep house with.

He did the handkerchief trick which would cause some good housekeepers to commit suicide. Where all the dirt came from is anybody's guess. "Did I consider myself a good housekeeper?" "Yes." "Did I realize all this filth was lurking in the rugs after I had cleaned just that morning?" "No." "Could I possibly face life without his cleaner?" "No." To this day, I don't know how it happened, but I bought his cleaner. He allowed me ten dollars on my old cleaner and every time I trudge up the stairs carrying the cleaner, I mentally kick myself for not keeping the other one for upstairs use. Life was beautiful until Norm came home the next week end and at the dinner table announced that we would move to

Maryland. We then discussed finances and he asked, "Did you spend any money this week, Bun?" I swallowed hard and said, "Yes, eighty-five dollars." The kids stopped chewing and Norm eyed his family then said, "I thought you weren't going to buy anything big until we decided what we were going to do." Bob came to my rescue and said, "It's nothing big Dad, it's just a vacuum cleaner." Norm cleared his throat and said, "By big, I didn't mean an elephant or the Brooklyn Bridge, I meant something expensive." We all laughed and started our digestive tracts working again and I promised Norm that I wouldn't make any more "big" purchases until he got a promotion.

Finding A Room In Aberdeen

In March of the year 1937, Norm received a rather chilly little form letter from the War Department telling him to report to Aberdeen Proving Ground at such and such a date. I was simply aghast at the idea and kept saying to Norm, "What would happen if you just didn't show up?" He eyed me in true soldierly disgust and answered me in an Ogden Nash fashion, "I've never seen a court martial, I hope I never see one, but I can tell you anyhow, I'd rather see than be one." I began to get the impression that he planned to answer the summons, so I asked, "How did you ever happen to take R.O.T.C. in college anyway?" "It was simple", he replied, "I merely substituted R.O.T.C. for a course in poetry" and I could tell from the far away look in his eyes that he was wondering if there had been any pretty girls taking the Omar Khayyam special, while he was out in the fields tripping in gopher holes learning the basic art of becoming an infantry officer.

Bob was boarding at Seminary that year and when some friends of ours volunteered to take Norma and Wade until school was out, Norm decided to take me to Aberdeen and just close up the house until summer.

We arrived in Aberdeen at dusk on a cold rainy night and spent several hours hunting for a room. We found lodging in a prefabricated shack which had obviously been hooked together a few days before we arrived. The rain came in without knocking and settled in pools on the bedroom floor. A baby wailed in the next room, so I crawled in the chimney bed and shed a few tears myself. The next morning, it was still raining and more water had come in unannounced, so Norm said, "Let's get out of this houseboat and find another place to stay." Talk about famous last words. For the next week we had to go back to the prefab and rest our weary bones. Aberdeen was definitely a broom town and every available room was rented out at fantastic prices. One night, we made our way to the Western Union office and prepared to wire the kids that I would be home soon because we couldn't find a place to stay. We wrote the wire and the operator read it back and then remarked that her husband had just left for active duty the day before and that she was planning to rent one room if we would eat out. Norm and I just stood there like a couple of Cigar Store Indians, speechless with delight at the prospect of boarding on dry land for a change. We went back to the houseboat and gathered up our belongings, paid the fabulous lodging fee, said, "Bon Voyage, happing sailing," and quickly departed.

We found Phoebe Thompson's house with much effort. Norm remarked to me that it looked well anchored, so we were soon established in our new home. Anyone who has ever lived in one room will probably sympathize with us, but it is something you have to experience yourself. Never are days as long as those in which you have absolutely nothing constructive or even destructive to do. I read until my eyes rebelled, knitted all sorts of unwearable objects, and drove around the countryside looking for old historic homes. The only one I ever located was the birthplace of John Wilkes Booth and I realize that any red blooded American would rebel at paying a quarter to go through the traitor's homestead, but being a lowly Canadian and not overly versed in Lincoln lore, I proceeded to pay the admission and looked over the establishment. You couldn't tell from looking at the old four post bed that it had witnessed the birth of Lincoln's assassin. A moth eaten old lady, one of Wilkes' descendents, was living in the house surrounded by photographs of John and the infamous Ford Theatre. No one had been there in over a year, so the old lady kept me there explaining that John hadn't really shot Lincoln. I guess she must have been very convincing as Norm and I went to a party on the Post that night, and Norm overheard me remark to his superior officer, that I didn't think John Wilkes Booth shot Lincoln after all. Norm suddenly decided that it was time for us to go home, but every time after that when I saw General Hatcher, he used to grin and ask me who I thought did shoot able Abe.

Thorn Meadow

Lieutenants Ferguson and Barth, who were Special Service officers in Norm's department, soon became fast friends of ours. We used to meet each evening for dinner, and I say dinner strictly out of kindness. There were numerous nasty little hovels masquerading under the name of restaurants, so we kept rotating thereby keeping one jump ahead of ptomaine poisoning. It was every evident that Duncan Hines had regurgitated rather than recommend the food to be had in Aberdeen. One night, we all drove into Baltimore to Miller's for seafood and the food was so clean and well-prepared that our stomachs rebelled and we all suffered a serious attack of indigestion. The next night found us back at one of our old haunts and Barth asked the lady in charge, what brand of starch she used. She told us and Norm suggested that she try Satina with it, as it made digestion so much easier.

Our conversation was almost as dismal as the food and Barth would always end up telling us about his wife and little girl. Fergie had a girl and wanted to get married, but had to find a place to live first, as there were no quarters available on the Post. Not too long after that, the men heard of a nice big old house that we could rent, if all three of us would chip in to pay the rent and buy the food. It sounded like a good deal to us, but I made the mistake of going to Williamsburg with Mother and when I returned, I found that Fergie had dashed away and married his lady love, Barth had rented his home and brought his wife and daughter down; and both couples were firmly entrenched in Thorn Meadow.

Thorn Meadow was one of the loveliest spots I have ever been in. I can't imagine how the owners ever left it in the first place. The house was fully furnished with beautiful antiques and the walls were spotted with numerous watery landscapes painted by the owner's wife. The main living room, which we never used, had two fireplaces and five sofas. Just off the front terrace, a spring had been dammed and formed a lovely swimming pool. It was a heavenly spot, but not for three such highly divergent families. The house was built on three levels, so naturally the first commers had taken over the two upper levels and left us the servant's quarters.

Fergie's wife had been married and divorced and had a little girl. The Barths had a little girl, and we had Norma and Wade down there for the summer with us. Loretta, the new bride, was a regular Kitty Foyle; pretty and smart and from a large family and had worked from the day she left high school. Polly had been raised in suburban Philadelphia, graduated from the Baldwin School, and then double crossed her mother by going in training to be a nurse. Polly was the soul of efficiency, but somehow managed to send out her laundry, read True Story magazines, sunbathe, and swim while Kitty Foyle and I staggered in and out of the laundry with baskets full of khaki uniforms. We suffered violent attacks of jealousy, whenever the laundry truck drove down to Thorn Meadow and the whistling driver left huge packages of clean clothes for the Barth family.

The kids told me that the Barths had colored toilet paper and matching soap and Kleenex, and one weekend when the Barths were away, I climbed up two flights to make a personal study of the psychology of pink toilet paper, but found that every door was locked, so that was when frustration set in. When they returned they had Polly's mother with them, and as she took an immediate dislike to Kitty Foyle and me, I was farther than ever removed from the pastel equipped master bath. Mrs. Ramsey and her dog both looked down heir noses at us when she announced that she lived on the Main Line, and neither Kitty nor I started to salaam or even take on a more reverent attitude. As for the pooch, neither Loretta nor I cared if he had sprinkled some of the best lawns in Bryn Mawr. We were waging our own private little war against snobbery and it killed Mrs. Ramsey to have to be polite to Norm, as he was her son-in-law's boss and outranked him.

One night Kitty and I returned into the library uninvited and found Polly and her mother sitting in chairs opposite each other reading by holding a magazine in one hand and tickling each other's foot with the other hand. We beat a hasty retreat and catalogued the Main Line as a good place to steer clear. Mrs. Ramsey cut her visit short and life returned to a more normal tempo. Polly really liked us, but her mother wouldn't let her while she was there. She should have known that Polly might get into bad company by marrying an athletic coach. After one month at Thorn Meadow, we were running on a reasonably smooth schedule, so we decided that a house warming was in order, and we each were allowed to invite two couples for a weekend. None of us realized what a riot it was going to turn into as we blissfully sent out the invitations to the housewarming to end all housewarmings.

The Housewarming

I can't remember who made out the shopping list for the housewarming at Thorn Meadow, but I do recall the list. It read something like this; one turkey, one case rye, one ham, one case of Scotch, Vienna bread, one case of bourbon, vegetables, four cases of beer, butter, case of ginger ale and sparkling water. I should have known by that list that the party would come to a bad end, but we were all optimistic as to the drinking capacity of our guests and friends.

Our weekend guests consisted of a highly successful career man and his artistic, temper mental wife. The other couple was strictly R.F.D. like Norm and I, so we had no problem there. Our artistic friend spent the day of the party arranging flowers in every possible container, including large tomato and pineapple juice cans which lent an air of festivity to the old homestead. It reminded me of geraniums growing in tin cans in farm house windows and never have I seen lovelier geraniums. You haven't lived until you have seen phlox springing from the top of a Dole pineapple juice can, or brown-eyed daisies eyeing you from bronze colored beer tins.

Polly had conceived the idea of having four colored boys from the Post Quartermaster Corps prepare and serve the buffet supper, as well as tend bar. We decided to use the ping pong table for the supper instead of moving the dining room table outside, so we had that set up out on the terrace. I had the makings of a memorable evening.

By four in the afternoon, all the guests had assembled on the terrace and we were anxiously awaiting the arrival of our husbands. They came roaring down the drive at five with cases of spirits jiggling merrily in the trunk; and were followed by a lumbering army vehicle full of food and good-natured colored boys to serve it. The bar was operating in no time at all and the ping pong table was soon groaning under the weight of all manner of good things to eat. I was parked in a deck chair engaged in a bit of faulty psychoanalysis when someone handed me a glass of scotch with orders to drink it and thereby determine whether it was fit for our guests to drink. I drained the glass and then paralysis set in and I was unable to leave the deck chair for the remainder of the evening. There was more activity and laughing and disorder than the old place had ever witnessed before. Norm would check up on me occasionally and was more than pleased to find me sitting quietly in the same chair. His invitation to play a game of badminton was greeted with an icy stare. One of Barth's guests decided it was high time Norm had something to drink and went in search of something non-alcoholic. He came upon a Dole pineapple juice can, but was slightly confused about the flowers.

After much deliberation, he removed the flowers, found a clean glass and confronted Norm in drunken triumph. It was dark on the terrace and Norm was flattered to think someone had found something to his liking; so took a long healthy swig of nondistilled flower water. It undoubtedly was a great shock to Norm as he reared up in the air and sputtered and his benefactor was in a state of near collapse. I tried to explain to Norm how it all happened, but he was already on his way to the bar and had the bar keep a generous amount of Scotch in the same glass and he gave it back to his new found friend. About that time, a ping pong game was in full swing and I watched dizzily as the small white ball danced around the turkey and ham. It was dark and late and the food was untouched. Not too long after that Norm said, "I think you'll go to bed now," and I was willing.

The next morning I was awake bright and early and was amazed to find Norm and Kitty saying goodbye to some people. Some wit had decided that a midnight swim was just what was needed, so most of the folks had taken a dip or else been thrown bodily into the ice cold water. The shock treatment had revived everyone sufficiently, so that the party had started all over again. I was furious to think I had missed all the fun. We found the four boys asleep under after game table and gave them coffee and sent them back to the Post with the truck. Needless to say, we spent the day washing glasses and sweeping the terraces as Norm had called to say the owner of the house was coming to call to see what kind of tenants we were, and that we should offer him some kind of refreshment, but not flower water. That night, we all sat out and watched the moon come up and Poly said wistfully, "That was really quite a housewarming," and Norm said, "What housewarming?" and it was so still we could hear as well as see the moon rise.

Three Couples Are A Crowd

The housewarming was soon a thing of the past and life was flowing along very smoothly considering the inmates of Thorn Meadow. There was a hint of fall in the air those cool nights and I, being the mother of three, was naturally the first to detect it. I was getting anxious for the time to come when Bob and Norma would be back in Kingston and safe within the portals of school. Wade of course, would remain with us which suited him perfectly, as he was still trying to make up for the missing out on the honeymoon; and a winter spent alone with us would give him a decided advantage over the other kids, or so he thought. I also realized that I would be more popular with the other girls if I had only one child to cope with. Hence, it was with no regret that Labor Day rolled around and we all took off to our various homes for the long weekend. Polly announced that "Mother" would be coming back with them for a few days and Kitty tried to look interested and wondered why she couldn't have gone down with the Titanic.

I should say in deference to "Mother", that she made a heroic effort to be nice to us poor mortals, mentioned the Main Line in only every third sentence, and confined foot tickling to the hour after which Kitty and I were apt to retire. You might almost say that visit was a social success. Such happiness, however, was short lived. We three girls had all undergone a great physical change, and our dispositions started to suffer as a result. We didn't make the horrible discovery until one day when we were all enjoying a dip in the ice cold swimming pool and Kitty remarked that we hadn't missed a day's swimming for a long, long time. We all looked at each other with accusing eyes and then made for shore like condemned women. We sat on the edge of the pool and dangled our feet in the water. Polly remarked wistfully that the very worst thing about being pregnant was not being able to see your own feet. I was strictly a novice at being pregnant, so asked the girls how you went about telling your husband. I never had approved of the Hollywood movie version in which the husband is always the last to know. Nor did I like the system in which Walter Winchell announced in his syndicated column that breakfast at home, let alone Sardi's, no longer appealed to him. I was all for a frank declaration of dependence and knew I could count on Norm for some encouraging, if not helpful advice. That night, with the immoral support of Polly and Kitty, I made my great announcement. Norm stopped snoring only long enough to say, "That so? I've had three myself and believe me, it doesn't hurt a bit. Goodnight Bun."

A couple of weeks later, Wade and Kitty's little girl started to school at Churchville and hence, a new morning routine was born. We had to get up earlier in the mornings, and there were lunches to be packed for Wade and Donna, once the men folk left for the camp. I think it was the strain of early rising that began to tell on us as we all started to get on each other's nerves. Donna never would eat anything, so we had our morning coffee to the tune of "Hurry-up and eat your cereal or you'll be late for school." Polly did everything with a lavish hand and it took at least four oranges to extract enough juice to keep scurvy from overtaking the small Barth child. Norm, unfortunately had read some where that the human body can only absorb so much orange juice and the rest was a complete waste. I think we are capable of assimilating about a tablespoon full; so this great waste on Polly's part bothered me. At home, Norm would count noses, then oranges. One morning in utter desperation, he mumbled to me that Polly's section of the Main Line must have been laid by William of Orange himself and old Ben Franklin had been receiving full credit for it all these years.

Polly and Loretta began to make long pilgrimages to Baltimore and I was left at Thorn Meadow with Marty, a young terror, if there ever was one. Polly always came home laden down with packages from Hutzler's. To my knowledge, the only purchases made by Kitty were at the fruit stalls in the famous Farmer's Market. She would buy this fruit to incorporate in Donna's lunch, thereby making the whole lunch more attractive to the child. Kitty would be packing sandwiches in the morning, then disappear to their wing of the house and return with some luscious bit of fruit and always made sure Wade's mouth was drooling before she popped it into Donna's lunch pail. Poor old Wade only had what the commissary on the post had to offer, but being a child of his father's, soon discovered that sitting near Donna at the lunch hour produced amazing results. Little did Kitty know that malnutrition was stalking Donna in the form of Wade Smith, who would in true Smith tradition, rather eat than anything else.

A week later, after the girl's had looked the heating system at Thorn Meadow over carefully, they began to hunt for a place to spend the winter. They were both city girls and the thought of a long, cold winter at Thorn Meadow didn't appeal to them. In no time at all they had located a singularly ugly little place in Harve De Grace, and gleefully announced that it was big enough for two families. Since we could not afford to pay the large rent and buy oil, too, we realized that we would have to leave Thorn Meadow. At the end of October we all moved, the Barths and the Fergusons to Harve De Grace, and the Smiths to Port Deposit.

New Housemates

Norm had a lucky break, as far as the house in Fort Deposit was concerned. A Captain Koenig had located the place, but his timid wife was afraid to stay alone all day long in the country, let alone the many nights he would be compelled to remain on the Post for duty. Besides, the rent was exorbitant for one couple and the sensible thing for them to do was to find a congenial couple to help pay the rent and share the commissary bill. That was where we came in. We had no letter of recommendation from our former allies and hoped the new family would overlook such a minor detail, especially with times as they were. They did and we were settled in our new environment in short order. Mrs. Richards, who owned the house, had taken an apartment in Baltimore for the winter due to gas rationing and the chance to make some money on the house. However, she left her big dog, Tack, there as he was not wanted in the apartment and besides his presence and reputation as a watch dog gave Mrs. Koenig false courage. We were happy about the arrangement as it gave Wade the companionship of a pet and Tack was a fine specimen of a dog and would have been most unhappy in the city.

The house itself was very impressive looking from the outside, but inside, it was one of the coldest, most formidable places I was ever in. All the walls were apartment house tan with vanilla colored woodwork. The kitchen was of white tile clinical vintage, and about as cheerful as a tomb. The only thing I really liked was the laundry shoot in our bathroom, which ended up in the cellar alongside the old washer. Since I was destined from the age of sixteen to do battle with dirty clothes forever, I loved that laundry shoot. Even the fact that Wade got stuck in the shoot didn't dampen my spirits. I caught up with him at the kitchen level and made him promise never to try the same trick in the incinerator slide. The novelty of dropping clothing down the shoot and disposing of garbage without leaving the kitchen, soon wore off and I decided to get acquainted with Mrs. Koenig.

It was several days before I knew they were the parents of a small baby girl. If Mrs. Koenig hadn't had a mania for boiling diapers, I might never have known about Mildred, but that was back in the days before Airwick appeared on the market and there is something undeniable about the odor of a well boiled diaper. Both the Captain and his wife were hell bent on making a chore rather than a pleasure out of parenthood, so Mildred was seldom in evidence. Norm, who was an old hand with babies, couldn't understand their obvious fear whenever Mildred exercised her lungs. Mrs. Koenig was rather pretty in a frightened sort of way and once I got to know her husband, I thought I knew why. He was a small blonde man with a mustache and Napoleon complex about his small stature, but what he lacked in size, he made up in culture. Before long there were maps of all the theatres of war tacked up in the den and every night we listened to the carious commentators and talked about current events. Besides keeping Mildred in boiled diapers, the Captain's lady was expected to read her Times from cover to cover each week and make intelligent remarks about labor, capital, and the world at large. If she wasn't right or expressed an opinion which didn't coincide with her husband's, he was hurt, depressed and immediately assumed the role of martyr. He would order her to bring him more coffee and the rest of the evening she was thoroughly unpopular. I lived in constant terror lest he ask me questions, so took to devouring the "United States News" as well as Time just in case. The mornings were almost as gruesome as the evenings. At breakfast, the Captain would outline the menu for dinner. Norm, who had never ordered a meal at home in his life, or even been consulted about one, was utterly fascinated by the procedure. I did the marketing, so listened carefully and made notes for future reference. One item the Captain lacked imagination about was dessert. All he wanted was pie every night. Every day was my pie day and not being overly fond of pie anyway, the days took on a horrible monotony. The Captain didn't like my crust and instructed his wife to teach me how to make decent crust, so while the diapers boiled merrily away on the stove, I learned the fine art of making pastry. One day Norm had to go to Washington for some special meeting and wanted me to go along.

"I can't really," I said. "Why?" he wanted to know and I said, "Because it's my day to make a pie." I was really in a rut.

I soon learned to dread Sundays, but for a different reason. The Captain was a pilot of sorts and near us was a seedy, little airport, which rented small battered aircraft to those foolish enough to pay the price. I could just see Mrs. Koenig's clothes allowance go up in the air every Sunday. One week, when I had done myself proud along the current events line and could fashion edible pie crust, the Captain invited Wade and me to accompany him to the airport. His wife, lucky devil, had Mildred as an excuse not to go. It was there that I had my first plane ride and it set me back twenty years in being air minded. We bumped along high above Chesapeake Bay for what seemed like hours, I got to thinking about how Norm was because he never ordered me to whip up a pie or go airplane riding with him. When we landed, I was in semi-coma and it was Wade's turn for a ride. I was too weak to object and as fate would have it, Wade found it to be a very satisfying experience. The next

Sunday I volunteered to stay home with Mildred and let Mrs. Koenig go joy riding with Napoleon. They agreed, so I stayed home, read Time and thought how narrowly I had escaped an early death.

Entertaining The Troops

The football season in Maryland brought us diversion from the diaper and pie routine. Norm had some friends at the Naval Academy in Annapolis, so one day Coach Tom Hamilton called and told Norm he could bring a few soldiers down for the Navy-Penn game. Back in those days, the Army hadn't fully recognized the crying need for organized recreation, so Norm served under the inspired title of "Morale Officer" and found entertainment as best he could for the men.

The invitation to Annapolis was wonderful, so Norm tacked a small notice on the bulletin board, saying that any boys who wanted to go to the game should apply at the Quartermaster depot for transportation. He expected a small response, but when two training battalions signed up, he became nervous, but nevertheless arranged transportation to Annapolis.

One night after Napoleon had given us a resume of the day's news, Norm casually remarked that we were going to a football game Saturday. "Just the two of us?" I asked. I couldn't remember ever having gone any place alone with Norm and the idea was a bit frightening. "No," he replied, "I'm taking a few soldiers along." I soon discovered that anything the American Army did was done in the grand manner. If more than one vehicle goes out on the highway, it becomes a convoy, and a convoy usually has a pace setter or leader and that was the position we found ourselves in that great day. In my maddest moments, I had never imagined that I would be going to a football game with forty, four-ton trucks following in my wake. By that time, I had assumed the shape of a penguin, but to quote Norm "not nearly as attractive" and the red plaid coat I owned was never intended to be worn by two people, but we wore it and went everywhere together that fall.

Norm pulled up in front of the assembled trucks, then got out to check up on the drivers and say a few words to the men which boiled down to, if any man dared say "sink the Navy" once we reached Annapolis, he would be tossed into the jug personally by Norm when they returned to Aberdeen. We roared on down the highway, all conversation being obliterated by the noise from the big trucks. I wanted to know how Norm could face Hamilton, but realized our first problem would be to get through the gates of the Naval Academy. The guard tried to give us a rough time and Norm was very polite, but it was nearing game time, so he finally had to emerge from the staff car, the mere act of Norm emerging from a car would terrify the average man, so the guard retreated into his little hut as Norm said, "Stand aside man, we're here on maneuvers."

Facing Tom was not quite as easy. He heard us approach long before he saw us and his face was a study. Norm looked a little sheepish as Tom eyed the convoy and said, "I hope you didn't forget anybody." Norm assured him that they had left a skeleton staff behind to keep the camp intact, and thanked Tom for inviting them down for the game.

The trip to Annapolis was such a success that Norm instigated sight-seeing trips to Washington. There were men from all over the United States at Aberdeen and many of them had never seen the Capital, so every Sunday we led a large convoy into the city and saw everything it had to offer. To me it was a wonderful way of escaping Sunday plane riding with Napoleon and Wade of course, stayed at Port Deposit so he could fly. The trips to Washington were really fun and we would get home at dusk and find the Koenigs waiting in the den for us. Through the courtesy of the "New York Times", the Captain had boned up on "The News of the Week in Review" and could hardly wait for me to remove my coat and reveal my ignorance as well as my figure, both of which were awe-inspiring. The Sunday pie was then unveiled and eaten with great relish on all our parts. Wade and Mildred were asleep and once the Russians were properly cussed out, we could, more or less relax.

On Sunday, December the Seventh, just the thousand of us were in Washington admiring the Lincoln Memorial when news of Pearl Harbor was released throughout the country. We were blissfully unaware of the fact until we returned to Port Deposit that evening. We found the

Captain with his ear glued to the radio looking like a stricken man. He kept mumbling "Pearl Harbor, damn Japs" and we thought he taken leave of his senses. The frightened one was the one to break the news gently to us and for once she outshone her husband. He couldn't believe that we had been knocking around Washington all day long and hadn't heard the news. He kept saying, "Just think you were in Washington at the time." Two hours later when Norm and I retired, I said from force of habit, "Just think you were in Washington at the time" and he replied, "Better Washington than Pearl Harbor. Tomorrow we'll be at war."

Nine Months and Counting

War was declared a few days later, but life went on at Fort Deposit much the same as it had prior to Pearl Harbor. We left for Rhode Island for the Christmas holidays after picking Bob and Norma up at school. I had decided that it would be the ideal time to tell the children about the possibility of a new baby being added to the family. I had asked Norm to help me out a bit, but should have known better. He said, "Don't you think the Bun has put on a lot of weight?" All agreed that I had and then he said, "Now tell them why" "We're going to have a baby," I announced and was greeted by a long silence. I glanced back at Norma, who sat there with a smug "only women can have babies look." Bob was thinking the situation over carefully and then said, "Just think, another mouth to feed." Wade was hurt to think that he was being replaced as baby of the family, it definitely was not the joyous moment I had anticipated. I began to wonder if it had been such a smart idea after all. I hoped my own family would be a little more enthusiastic about the whole affair. Mother was so pleased at the prospect of having a little granddaughter to dress, but Norm soon put an end to that by informing her that I was going to have a boy, in other words, Norm had already made up his mind about that. Norm took a plane back to Aberdeen for a week and then came back to Rhode Island to drive the children back to school and us to Port Deposit. Meanwhile the folks who were living in our house decided to move, so we announced to the Koenig's that I would go back to Pennsylvania and live in our own place with Wade. It was rather a sad parting, as we had grown quite fond of one another. The Koenig's were going to look for a place in town, and thus we parted. Coming back to Huntsville was quite an adjustment to make. We missed Norm, but at least the children could come home weekends and Norm managed to get home quite frequently. I found a new friend in Huntsville who was in rare form, too, so we palled around together and had a lot of fun together. This girl set a great store by walking and practically every day would call and announce that we were going for a walk. For those who believe in Mothers marking their children, it would be safe to say that we each have a potential marathon winner in our family circle. We traveled over hill and vale usually accompanied by Arline's cocker spaniel, with Airline at the other end of the leash. That beast would never hurry until he got on ice and then he delighted in hurrying Arline over that. I tremble to think what might have happened if she had fallen. We were good for each other inasmuch as we would each look at the other one and think "I couldn't possibly look as bad as she does." We both wore mangy old fur coats and it was a good thing hunting season was over or we never would have come out of the woods alive.

Arline, by virtue of a Caesarian Birth, had her child eight days before I had mine. It was a beautiful little female with curly hair and pink, not red, complexion. Norm came home the following weekend and we went over to the Elickers to spend Saturday evening. Jane took one look at me and said, "You better go to the hospital." If I knew then what I know now, I would have waited until the following morning, but being new at this baby business, I went early and suffered long. Norm occupied a Morris chair in my room and his snores kept time with my groans. About midnight I took an intense disliking to the man occupying the Morris chair. By now, I hated him. Like most women in labor, my mind began to review my life. Why was I ever born? Heck that was easy to solve. It was because my Mother had been fool enough to get herself in a similar condition. Were you ever going to have any more children? I should say not. In fact, you had already decided never to sleep with the occupant of the Morris chair again. Where was that fool doctor anyway? Never could stand the man anyway. Here comes a nurse. All we need now is another nurse to come in and look at you and then at her watch. Why doesn't the stupid fool do something besides gaze at her Hamilton? Couldn't she give you a knock-out drop? Oh no, not her. She believes in the old Bible saying, "Six days shall thou labor," and you in the bed can just wait till Sunday for all she cares. Let's see, when is Sunday? Should you go home and come back later. You turn to consult the sleeping, but decide why bother. Sleep on brother; we'll catch up with you on the two o'clock bottle schedule. There must be some way of getting even. The night nurse wears herself out and dawn comes blasting into the room as a new nurse raises the shade. All hospitals seem to be run alike. One set of nurses knock themselves out getting you washed and to sleep only so a fresh crew can come bouncing in the morning to awaken you. The new nurse asked timidly if I wanted to brush my teeth. I replied that I had merely stopped in the night before to have a baby and that I wasn't' the least bit interested in brushing my teeth. In fact, I was quite sure I had gnashed them to death during the long night, so why bother. Norm awakened and asked, "That you Bun?" and I replied, "Well it isn't Betty Grable." You can't guess who came in then. The doctor himself, looking not at all concerned about my suffering. With him were several nurses who eyed me with distaste and then consulted their graduation Gruens. They shook their heads and left. Later, I found out that that one's pains must be synchronous with the ticking of the Gruens or the delivery room would have none of you. The morning wore on and about noon time a sadistic grin spread over the nurse's face. It seems that the Gruen and I were at last in complete harmony with each other. I suffered the indignity of being dressed in long white stockings and having my head wrapped up in a towel and then I was on my way. Norm told me goodbye and said he'd be around when I got back. By then a shot of something they had jabbed into my arm began to take effect and I forgot how much I disliked the man I was saying goodbye to. In fact, for a man, he wasn't too bad.

Punchy Arrives And Norm Goes To War

In less than an hour, I was back in my room feeling ten years younger and twenty pounds lighter. Norm was smiling happily and said, "I just knew you'd have a boy, Bun." I was thinking to myself, what chance would my poor little genes have anyway, but didn't want to give Norm the satisfaction of knowing what I was thinking about. I felt tired and sleepy and thought that as soon as Norm left, I would go to sleep and sleep indefinitely. Norm had other plans, however. "Sit up Bun," he said, "Come on Bun, sit up. I'm going to comb your hair." I replied that I didn't want my hair combed. He said, "You're going to have your picture taken now and your hair looks like it's been slept in." Surely, he must be jesting. I sat up and he fixed my hair using the same tactics one would in grooming a horse. He decided that he would braid it so I wouldn't look quite so much like a witch and from the pictures we have as evidence, the result was gruesome. The photographer arrived and then Bob and Wade arrived and then I suggested that I would like to see the newly arrived child. Just then the nurse came in and placed the child beside me and the photographer went into action. I gave him my best forced smile. After the last flash, I finally got a good look at the little demon that had caused me such an uncomfortable night. I noted with delight that he had not inherited the Smith nose, which is in my mind, second only to the Hapsburg jaw. Norm kept saying, "Look at those hands Bun, they really will be able to handle a football." In fact, he was too intrigued with the child's large hands that the telegrams he sent to our families read, "Phyllis gave birth to a pair of hands." Mother had her wits about her and wired back, "Wonderful news for Ripley. Hope he or she has head and body to go with them."

At long last they all left me alone, but before Norm left he asked, "What are you going to do now, Bun?" I didn't make known to him my fondest desire, but replied, "Oh I'm just going to lie here and look at my feet. I haven't seen them in months you know," so he departed happy in the knowledge that I wasn't going to fritter away the afternoon in a semi- coma. I was soon off slumber dreaming about a wonderful country where the men had all the babies, and the women slept in Morris chairs.

The ten day sojourn in the hospital dragged by and by that time Norm had reconciled himself to the fact that I was unable to nurse the child who had by that time been named, then nicknamed "Punchy". It looked as if poor Punchy would have to seek nourishment elsewhere. Norm tried everything in his power to make an Elsie Borden out of me, but finally gave up and said, "It's like trying to get blood out of a turnip. Just think of all the bottles and all that mess." I was sorry about the whole thing, but couldn't see any reason in becoming morbid about it, so suggested that Norm lay in a supply of Carnation before I went home.

Two days later after my homecoming, Norm was summoned to Indiantown Gap and at that time of the war, it meant only one thing. The Gap was a point of getting men ready for embarkation. I went to the Gap with Norm fully expecting to spend a few days at Hershey with him, but Uncle Sam had other plans. Once we arrived there, Norm was confined to an enclosure to receive shots and then leave the country. It was the most helpless sensation I have ever known, saying goodbye to him through the barb wire fence. He kept telling me to take good care of the kids and not to worry about him, I drove home in a daze and found the kids all home looking out for their new little brother. There was a formula to be made, diapers to be washed and a dinner

It seemed like forever until the first letter from Norm arrived. All mail was heavily censored, so he couldn't tell us much about what was going on, except that they were on the high seas and headed for somewhere. He ended his letter by telling me to take good care of the kids and the furnace. Those two lines became stock phrases of his and in every letter I ever received; I was cautioned about the kids and the furnace. Soon after that, V Mail was invented and I am sure Norm wrote me every day he was overseas. That year seems more or less a nightmare to me as I think back on it. It was a good thing we all had Punchy to think about. He had the undivided attention of all the kids and as time wore on, he improved somewhat in looks, The fact that he was no beauty bothered Wade more than a little bit. He used to mow Arline's lawn and in this way saw a lot of her little daughter and was able to compare the two babies and how they were developing. Ellen was a beautiful baby. One day, Wade said to Arline, "You're baby may be prettier, but our baby is smarter," and that has become a classic with us.

Along about August, we had a letter from my Mother saying she was coming to visit as she was most anxious to see her little grandson. This was definitely a crisis, so we held a family consultation as how to let Nana first view her little grandson. Bob allowed that he thought evening would be the ideal time for Nana to arrive, as her first viewing of Punchy would be bottoms up and from that angle, he looked pretty cute. Wade suggested that he wear a bonnet to cover his head and Norma got mad and said, she thought we all were just terrible. She thought Punchy was lovely and knew Nana would too. Mother arrived in the afternoon and we all went down to meet her. She gathered the small bundle of flesh in her arms, looked him over carefully and remarked, "Why Phyllis Oxley, he's a cute little scamp." This convinced me that the old saying about beautiful being in the eyes of the beholder was more than true.

Things were going along beautifully until the phone rang one day and it was the Walkathon girl herself asking us to come up for lunch and horrors; bring Punchy along with us. We went and after lunch, put the babies on a blanket out in the sun and watched them as only new mothers can watch babies. Arline remarked that she thought Punchy looked a lot like my Mother. It came as rather a shock to Mother who was thinking right along that he must take after Norm's side of the family. When we went home, I took Bob aside and told him what Arline had said. He looked very smug and said, "I knew he didn't take after our side of the family."

Two weeks ago, I was in the office of the school Punchy goes to. The girl working there looked at Punchy and turning to me said, "Is he a Smith?" I said, "Yes, why?" "Oh, I just knew it; he looks exactly like Bob." We haven't reported this to Bob yet. I wonder what his "other mouths to feed" are going to look like?

Try To Choke Me, Bun

September came and the kids went back to school. Punchy and I stayed home and took care of the furnace. Christmas would have been a grim affair except for Punchy. The boys set the train up for him around the tree and he was fascinated by it. Mother came for the holidays and we did manage to make a fairly happy Christmas for the family. Norm, by that time, had landed in Oran and we had all kinds of unusual greeting cards from him. A telegram came from him, too, on Christmas day which made us very happy. We wondered where he was and whether or not his Christmas package had reached him in time. We had sent him a fantastic watch which was waterproof, shockproof, dustproof and bombproof. In fact, the salesman assured me that if the wearer was blown to bits, the watch would still be intact. I assure you that was a great source of comfort to me, especially when we read in the paper a few weeks later that Norm was injured and in an army hospital. All I ever knew about Norm's army career was what I read in the papers. He wrote later on that he had a neck full of shrapnel, but like he said, it was lucky it was his neck. Norm has the biggest neck I have ever seen. He gives all credit for its size and strength to a series of correspondence courses he took in his youth from one Farmer Burn's. I guess Farmer Burn's was the Charles Atlas of his youth. This course dealt mostly with exercises to strengthen the neck. At the end of the first week, Norm challenged a friend at school to try and choke him. Rome wasn't built in a day and neither was Norm's neck. When the principal found them, Norm was lying unconscious on the playground, eyes bulging, and face purple and breathing in gasps. From that day forward Norm resolved to develop a neck that no one could ever wring, whether in fun or desperation. To this day, the most endearing thing Norm can say to me is, "Come on Bun, try and choke me." I will admit there have been several times during our marriage that I could have done so joyfully, but he never chooses those moments to invite me to. One night we were at the sink finishing up the dinner dishes when a sudden wave of affection for the little woman overcame him and he said, "Come on Bun, try and choke me." I dried my hands on my apron and tried my darnedest to choke him. Suddenly a knock came at the back door, and as we were standing beneath the dazzle of a hundred watt bulb, there was no mistaking what I was up to. I stole away into the other room and let Norm go to the door. After our caller left, still bug-eyed from the revolting demonstration he had witnessed, Norm roared, "Come back here and finish choking me." Later, he wanted to know why I had run out on him and I replied, "Well, I couldn't very well have gone to the door and said, come in Sir, while I choke my husband, could I?" and he admitted that it would have sounded a bit silly.

In February we saw in the paper that Norm was planning to fly back to this country, but the plans went awry. It turns out that he was already to board the plane, when the authorities discovered that he himself weighed more than was allowed for a man and his luggage. He took a ship home. I almost said boat, but have been corrected so many times by Bob and Wade, both nautical young men, that I occasionally remember and say ship, which is correct. We watched the papers for further news of Norm's progress home, but didn't see anything to indicate just when he would arrive. One evening the phone rang. I answered and it was a call from Yew York. The conversation ran something like this. "Hello Bun." I answered, "Hello." "How are you?" "Fine, how are you?" "I'll be home on the two-fifteen tomorrow, goodbye." I said, "Goodbye." The kids asked me who called and I said, "Dad." I just couldn't believe that Norm was coming home.

We all met the train that famous Sunday. Punchy was looking less like the combination of a bald eagle and tired crow every day. In fact, we were all pleased with his progress. Norm got off the train and I was speechless. I had forgotten how big he was and to add to his huge stature, he was wearing an English army trench coat which completely enveloped him. An overseas cap was perched on his head at a rakish angle and he looked just wonderful. He picked Punchy up and said, "He's not very big Bun." Norma was on the defensive and said, "He's not a year old yet, give him time." "What the devil," said Norm, "I weighed more than that when I was born." None of us doubted that statement and Norm hustled off to get his baggage lined up. We drove on home and had dinner, then sat around talking and looking at each other in an unbelieving manner. For the first time in my life, I realized how Mother must have felt when Mr. Micawber returned from some of his jaunts. Norm had brought me a painting of a girl which I just love. He had seen it in a shop window and he said it reminded him of me. Anyone who has seen the picture agrees that Norm got home at the right time. She was looking fairer to him every day.

That night after all the kids had retired; Norm looked at me and said, "Come over here." I walked over to where he was sitting and he said, "Try and choke me Bun."

Balancing The Checkbook

I have always been glad that I was completely honest with Norm about my lack of understanding arithmetic. I admitted to him that I took Algebra Two three times and wouldn't have passed it the third time, if the boy who sat in front of me hadn't been enamored with me and sat in a position that made copying from his paper reasonably easy. Besides the teacher was getting pretty sick of my dumb algebra face. English had always been my favorite and best subject. I remember in grammar school, I told my long-suffering teacher that I planned to write a book some day and she replied that with my imagination, it should be a cinch. I started a novel that summer, but it died before long. In high school I had one teacher who encouraged me. His name was Elmer Smith and he appreciated my attempts to be humorous on the taxpayer's paper. Every now and then he would say, "That's pretty good Oxley," and his words were music to my ears. He wasn't being rude calling me by my last name. It was the rage when I was in high school to call male and female alike by his last name. I couldn't help it because mine was such a horrible one. From Smith's class I went on to a Miss MacPhearson. She was a good looking red head who had just been through some horrible ordeal that summer. She was either on a boat that had caught on fire, or one that was grounded, I can't exactly remember, but we spent a great deal of time in talking over her harrowing experience. I did what might be termed a satire of her narrow escape from the clutches of death and from then on Oxley was not the teacher's pet. I knocked myself out writing themes that winter, but never got higher than a C. I did manage a C plus on a theme about Mussolini. She called me in after class and said she liked it, and then asked me where I copied it from. I had gathered my revolutionary information from the Italian neighborhood I lived in and to this day I believe she thinks me guilty of plagiarism. So much for my English.

The one thing that worried Norm about leaving the country was leaving me in charge of the family finances. He hauled me down to the bank shortly before he left, and introduced me to a Mr. Evans. He had deemed Mr. Evans to be an understanding soul who would see that my account wasn't overdrawn more than once a month. I must say that he proved a staunch friend all during my banking years. Norm's Army check went directly to the bank the first of every month and repairs were promptly made on my account.

One day I was in Scranton with a friend shopping and needed some money, so dashed over to a bank to cash a check. I had no means of identifying myself, so the man I was talking to asked if I minded if he called the bank back home. I said no, of course not, but told him to ask for Mr. Evans. The call went through and in no time at all Mr. Evans was on the other end of the line. The man stated his business and there followed a long pause. I then overheard Mr. Evans' harassed voice ask, "What is she doing in Scranton?" "Shopping I guess, do we cash the check or don't we?" "Sure, sure", boomed Mr. Evans' voice, "tomorrow's the first."

It took Norm the better part of a month to get the trusty checkbook in order. I had managed to miscalculate three hundred dollars and it took Norm quite a while to catch up with it. He would moan and groan and remark, it was a darn good thing he came home when he did. I was overawed at his ability to make order out of chaos and kept complimenting him on his mental viewpoint about the whole thing. He wrote a long involved letter to Mr. Evans and let me read it. It was a masterpiece and managed to say very nicely to Mr. Evans that he really appreciated them all being so decent to me while he was away. Between the lines, however, one could detect a faint "thank you for keeping Phyllis out of the clink."

One month of being docile and hanging my head in shame went a long way and I soon became tired of being the underdog. There came a time when the children questioned me about things and I would say, "Go ask Einstein, he's right in the living room." The cold war didn't last forever as Norm was sent to Lexington. I will admit that he took the checkbook with him and volunteered to be bookkeeper for the entire family. As he was leaving, he eyed me and said, "You're such a nice girl, it's a shame you haven't a head for figures." I said, "I suppose you think you have a head for figures." He smiled wickedly and said, "I sure do." "I know you do," I replied, "but how's your math?"

Norm The Bass Drummer

Norm was very happy with his assignment in Lexington. He came home around Easter time and we all drove down to Lexington to see the town and where Norm was living. When we arrived in Lexington, Norm grabbed Punchy and dashed into Ashburne's tourist home with him and if I hadn't sent Bob in after him, he'd be in there yet. We were waiting in the car and felt it was no time for Norm to have such a highly paternal spell overtake him. The Ashburn's welcomed us with true southern hospitality and we could see that Norm was well taken care of. We went home after Easter and left Norm in Lexington with no misgivings whatsoever. Bob had his driver's license at that time and I was counting on him to help on the long drive home. Before we had gone too far, he announced that when he got back to school he had lots of bookwork to do and must rest his eyes. You know who drove the tribe home; Mother of course.

That summer a friend and I went down to visit Norm. At that time, the joint was really jumping. The Army had really moved in and as near as my weak brain could figure out, there were two definite factions battling one another. I wasn't there long enough to take sides, but knew that I was on the athletic side in case of a showdown. There was so much intrigue going on that Stalin could have picked up a few pointers. Be that as it may, my friend and I had a gay time. The Athletics and Recreation Dept. had organized a band, reputedly the only all-officer band in the country. They were shy of a base drummer and Norm in a jovial moment announced that he could play the bass drum. The leader of the band was a serious young man and believed Norm. Marian and I were a little nervous about the whole affair when we realized that Norm meant to go through with the gag. The band had several rehearsals, all of which Norm managed to evade, and then the fateful afternoon arrived.

The band assembled and sure enough Norm was in the starting lineup with a large drum hanging around his middle. They had their pictures taken and then the concept began. Whenever we least expected it, a loud explosion would rent the air. The band leader practically fainted on the podium and people around us began to twitch and mutter, "Who in hell is that bass drummer?" and make other equally kind remarks. Marian and I stayed glued to our chairs in fascinated horror. The leader became desperate and gave Norm the signal to stop. Norm mistook the signal as a come-on and really beat the living daylights out of that big drum. Finally the concert ended. Norm had had the time of his life, and since he outranked everyone who played with him or complained about his poor timing, he remained in the band. Marian and I left town before another concert was played, but a friend wrote us that the first one had been child's play compared to the second. Seems Norm had thrown in a little boogie beat that threw everyone out of time and he ended the concert in a triumphant boom all by himself.

That fall Norm prevailed upon me to spend the winter in Lexington with him. I found out first that the band had disbanded, so felt it was safe to walk along the streets of the town with the Colonel.

Anyone who has ever lived in a boarding house with a young child can well appreciate the kind of winter I spent. Punchy had learned to walk, so I had to stake him out on the front lawn while I bent over the bathtub to wash his diapers. Mr. Ashburne took pity on me and let me use their decrepit old washing machine and we became fast friends. He loved to go to auctions and took me to several, way out in the country. Mr. Ashburne could not resist buying canned fruit to serve to his borders. At one place he purchased some peaches that should have joined AA long before appearing on Mr. Ashburne's table. Norm partook heavily of dessert that night and reeled away from the table. He admitted to me later in the evening that that was the closest he had ever been to being intoxicated. "You dog, why didn't you tell me they were so good?" I inquired and he said, "Now Bun, remember your condition."

We had discussed at length the idea of another Smith. My argument was that I wanted a companion for Punchy, but Norm knowing the way of the world said, "What you mean is someone for Punchy to fight with," and sure enough he was right again.

Last summer we drove through Lexington in the convertible and stopped at Ashburn's. We hadn't there five minutes before the phone rang and a friend of Mrs. Ashburne's said to her, "I just saw Colonel Smith drive through town." "I know," said Mrs. Ashburne, "He's here now." It's nice to know that kind of people.

Jasper And The Fire Bombs

When Jasper, as we promptly nicknamed him, called on the secretary of the Jackson Township Volunteer Fire Department, he almost made a sale. If I hadn't been in the living room frantically ironing organdy curtains, he would have sold Norm enough carbon tetrachloride bombs to smother a fire in the Empire State building.

Punchy came in to tell me I was wanted out on the porch; so I pranced out to see why I was needed. Norm introduced me to Jasper and with that Jasper started his routine which started with the Chicago fire and ended with more recent disasters. He asked me if I had read about the couple who left their four small children in bed ....went to the movies .... and returned to find the children burned beyond recognition. By that time I was conflagration happy, so replied, "That could never happen to us. In the first place, we never go to the movies and in the second place; we don't have four small children. Will you kindly excuse me? I left the iron on in the living room."

No sooner had those last words kissed my larynx goodbye than I deeply regretted them. Jasper grew livid, turned to Norm and said, - "Hear, hear – so you couldn't possibly have a fire. I hate to say this, Mr. Smith, but I don't feel that your wife is a very sympathetic woman." I came back into the house and found the iron ticking merrily away, so finished off the curtains. I could hear Norm saying goodbye in far too cozy a fashion, and asking Jasper to return some evening that week with samples.

He came on in and said, "Now Bun, I've always wanted more fire protection than we have and this looks good to me." No response. "Jasper says Arch Brooks wouldn't be without his," "His what?" I asked absent mindedly. "His carbon tetrachloride bombs," Norm replied and sighed and left the room. "Where are you going?" I asked. "To get some ice coffee," was the sad reply. "Oh" I said, "I thought perhaps you were going to call Bob Rinehimer and cancel your fire insurance." "Don't be a goose," he said and we dropped the subject.

Fate played right into Jasper's hands. The next day we read in the paper of the Hazleton tragedy in which five brothers were burned to death. The sad news was just like a hypo for Jasper who came back that night armed for the killing. He had a dog-eared edition of the Record tucked under one arm and his life-saving kit under the other. He and a bat came in together, so I screamed, made tracks for the laundry, and slammed the door. I heard Jasper remark that he knew I was that sort of a person, "scared to death of a bat," he said, "but doesn't worry about her house or children burning." Meanwhile, Jasper was firmly entrenched in the living room. He was showing Norm a sample of the bomb and what held it up when I joined them. "Just think," he said, "with seven of these in the living room, a fire wouldn't have a chance." However, his company didn't do things halfway. They had to outfit the whole house, including cellar and attic. Each bomb ran about six dollars, so I did some sloppy mental arithmetic and figured that for somewhere in the neighborhood of three hundred dollars, we could be reasonably combustible and told Jasper so. Jasper packed his kit, shook hands with Norm and left with the air of a disappointed undertaker. "No sale," I said to Norm, "He looked a little burned up, don't you think?" And he agreed with me.

Later that week, he called on Paul Gross at the Coal-o-matic. He told Paul how Mrs. Smith had ruined a sale for him because she didn't like the looks of bombs dangling in every room in the house. Paul wasn't giving Jasper too rough a time and things were going smoothly when Marcia spoke up and said, "If Mrs. Smith doesn't like the looks of the bombs, I'm sure Mrs. Gross won't." Jasper turned on her and asked, "And precisely how do you know whether or not Mrs. Gross will like this manner of saving life and property?" Marcia smiled and reiterated, "She happens to be my mother. "

" And I still claim that if Mrs. Smith doesn't like the looks of them, Mrs. Gross won't." And you wonder why salesmen die young!

No More Reunions

This is one of those nights in which Norm realizes he didn't marry superwoman after all. He seems to take my literary (if I may abuse the word) career far more seriously than I do. In fact, it is he who beats me into writing an article each week which will sadly deflate those who feel sorry for him.

Last Sunday we left for Asheville, North Carolina to attend an Army reunion. I found that a reunion of Army officers is second cousin to a college reunion and which is more trying. I have yet to decide. Norm insisted upon taking me to his twenty year college reunion. We arrived on the campus early in the morning all set to have a wonderful time. The first man Norm ran into hailed him in a jovial voice and each proceeded to put the other's right hand out of commission with ye olde Theta Chi handshake. Finally, the newcomer introduced himself, and Norm's response has become a family byword. "I thought you looked familiar." I was sitting in the car viewing the Smith profile and thinking how nice it was for two brothers to be so very, very close, that one had to introduce himself to the other.

The girls were something else again. The married ones were plump and contented looking. The unmarried ones were scrawny and discontented looking. They all sat there and thought how old looking the others were getting. No one could really get excited about the class song, but a feeble attempt was made to make it heard throughout the dining hall. I was eyed with great suspicion by those who remembered Smith, a four letter man in his college years. Following the luncheon we were taken on an inspection tour of the campus, which as far as I could see consisted of trailers, Quonset huts and Curity diapers. All you had to do to be considered intelligent was to mutter occasionally, "My my, but hasn't the old place changed" and I ran that into the ground. That night we went to a dance and I was shoved around the dance floor by Norm's buddies of old and I couldn't help but wonder why girls hated to be wall flowers. I vowed I would never attend another reunion.

The Army reunion is now a thing of the past. It was all instigated by one Ed Denton, a great basketball player in his youth. He, Norm and Danny Yates were stationed in Asheville at one time during the war and a fine time was had by all. The three of them were interested in sports and were known throughout Asheville as the "Three Musketeers." The army had taken over Asheville and the townspeople were helpless to do anything about it. The three buddies dashed madly from tennis court to golf course to basketball floor and any poor civilian who got in their way regretted his folly. The whole town began to look like the location for the Olympic tryouts. Somebody had to do some paper work, so three good looking girls were hired to type and arrange dances, frankfurt roasts and tours of the Smokey Mountains.

Ed was very adept at filching commissary steaks, so the girls were hired for their ability to cook as well as type. Our first big shock was to hear that the hotel room would be ten dollars a night. Secondly, Uncle Sam would not be supplying free steaks. How times had changed. We arrived in town only to find that Denton would not arrive until the next morning and that Yates wasn't planning to arrive until the weekend. We hiked ourselves over to one of the ex-secretary's apartments and in no time at all had been invited to a Southern fried chicken dinner.

The next day we just missed Denton by five minutes. He had arrived in town, checked into the hotel and was last seen by the desk clerk leaving the hotel with his golf bag and two men. We drove out to the Biltmore Country Club and watched most of the afternoon for him to arrive on the ninth hole. He never did arrive for the simple reason that he played at the Asheville Country Club. That night we caught up with him in his room at the hotel and he insisted that we all go to the Sky Club for dinner. He was terrifically happy to see the Colonel, but eyed me with obvious distaste. He had left his wife back home in Indiana and promised to take her to Chicago once he had returned from Asheville. We went to the Sky Club and then the great basketball player disappeared and we didn't see him again until the morning we left Asheville. Danny Yates and his pretty little wife arrived the night before we left, so we did get to see them. I enjoyed the trip, but can't help but feel it was a lousy reunion.

We came home Friday night and the little boy next door came running over and calmly announced that someone had taken my station wagon. We didn't believe him until Norm yanked the barn door open. Sure enough it was gone. Furthermore, the juvenile Sherlock Holmes had heard someone in our house at dinner time and rushed over to tell his Grandmother. By the time she reached out yard the station wagon was leaving the yard with two men in it. Norm and I were completely baffled. I took my suitcase upstairs and discovered that Wade had come home unexpectedly, let himself in the dining room window, and was on his way down to Walters for dinner accompanied by young Bob when our neighbor saw him. I was relieved, but could have cheerfully wrung his neck for not leaving a note.

Yesterday we washed, mowed an acre of lawn, froze chickens, picked beans in Clint Ide's garden and froze them and Norm asked if I had written anything for the Post. I ignored the question. Tonight he asked me again and this is what happened.

A New Hampshire Visit

Way back in the good old days before I became involved with Smith, Inc., I used to spend the summers in New Hampshire with an aunt and uncle of mine. A good friend of my uncle's owned two houses near Center Sandwich and used to rent the little Cape Cod cottage to my uncle and kept the other for his own use and for entertaining friends who like to spend their vacations gazing at the mountains.

I was ten at that time and not worldly enough to wonder who our landlord's hostess was on various weekends. We knew her by sight and name, but beyond that, were ignorant as to whence she came and whither she went. She was undoubtedly the homeliest woman I have ever seen and always wore a picture hat and flowing chiffon garments. Most of her time was spent at an antiquated sewing machine whipping up all kinds of horrible looking curtains and bedspreads for the two houses.

She was rewarded in later years when Mr. Witherspoon died and left her one house in New Hampshire and one along the Rhode Island shore. Unfortunately, she remained at the shore place after Labor Day in the year of our Lord 1939 and was washed away, sewing machine and all, by the hurricane.

When her will was found, my uncle became the owner of her place in New Hampshire and the little house was left to another man.

Just before the war, I inveigled Norm up to New Hampshire with the idea in mind of buying the little house which was up for sale at the time. He refused, so I gave up the idea of a summer place in New Hampshire. However, I was determined that if I ever had any children I would see that they spent some time in New Hampshire every summer and get to know and love that beautiful state as I did.

Twenty years ago, that part of New Hampshire had not suffered a real estate boom and our pet diversion was picnicking and exploring old deserted homes. Now you can picnic, but all the old houses have been purchases and remodeled according to the taste of the new owners. There are only a few families around who have been summering there as long as my aunt and uncle.

I was pleased to find that Professor Frankfort of Yale was still on deck this summer and availing himself of the rare N.H. air. As kids we were afraid of him, but held him in high esteem as he was what is nowadays called a "brain" and mother always ranked great thinkers in a class of their own. One day, we kids were playing hop scotch in the dirt road in front of the house when Professor Frankfort drove in view clothed in what was undoubtedly the first model Jantzen ever put on the market. My brother whispered, "Here comes old hot dog himself," and we snickered, but froze in horror when the great man himself stopped by us and showed us a lizard he had found reposing beneath a rock. After the biology lesson he went on down the road thinking his own thoughts and never spoke to us again for the next twenty years.

This summer he was cornered by my aunt in the middle of Bear Camp Pond and was forced into acknowledging an introduction to Norm. Aunt Stella had devised a clever way of introducing Norm to the summer folk. As the woods were full of professors and retired Army men, she introduced Norm to professors as Professor Smith and when confronted by an old Army reject, she would introduce him as Colonel Smith.

On the fateful day I refer to, both men were halfway across the pond, but still not in water above their middles. I was going to say waistline, but in either case, it would be a rank distortion of fact. Aunt Stella, who must have been underwater, suddenly appeared and caught Professor Frankfort unaware and introduced Norm to him. I think he asked, "What college" and as Norm's answer had nothing to do with the Ivy League, he was given a fast brush off.

Professor Frankfort made for shore, and joined his wife and secretary who were busy with pads and pencils. Whether he was dictating the great American novel making formulas for splitting atoms, we didn't know, but the women hung on his every word. Mother then told me that Professor Frankfort was all wrapped up in atomic energy and was soon to leave for Mexico to study eons or peons and possibly hunt for uranium on the sly.

When Norm joined us on the beach, I told him the little bit I knew about the man and he was quite unimpressed and said, "That guy should incorporate a little energy, atomic or otherwise, into his handshake." As we sat there drying our suits, I must have done a little thinking, always a painful process, so I said to Norm, "You know something," and he quickly replied, "I don't know anything." I started in all over again. "I was just going to say that I would hate to be married to a brainy man like Professor Frankfort." By that time the professor had dried sufficiently what I thought t to be the same old Jantzen and left the beach followed by the scribblers. We watched him depart and I said to Norm, "Doesn't he inspire you? Norm yawned and said, "I can hardly wait to get to Abercrombie's and buy a Geiger counter," and then proceeded to fall asleep in the hot midday sun.

Roughriders

I have never ceased to marvel at the way many old New England farmhouses were built. There is really nothing too revolutionary about the ranch house trend when one takes into consideration the homes of the rugged Yankees. Everything including barn, woodshed, tool house and you know what else was under one roof and in inclement weather, all functions of every day life could be carried out without once leaving the premises. It was this type of place that my uncle inherited.

With all due respect to him and the late Mr. Witherspoon, I would like to state that under that roof was housed the world's worst collection of old dejected beds. The dormitory in which we were lodged would have been the ideal spot in which to organize the society for the prevention of cruelty to old mattresses. In a little room off the dormitory was an old horror we dubbed "the hammock". We promptly gave Wade the dubious honor of sleeping in there alone. His father allowed that an old Coast Guardsman should get used to sleeping in a hammock anyway. The younger Smiths were put to bed in a contraption resembling the surf rolling in at Coney Island and Norm and I got the lucky number, a battered studio couch.

The first night there we were putting the boys to bed when I noticed a dashing picture of Mr. Witherspoon taken in his youth when he was a rough rider in Buffalo Bill's Wild West Show. It started a long train of memories as far as I was concerned, and I proceeded to tell Norm about my Uncle Sid who I hadn't thought of for a great many years. Uncle Sid was a rough rider in Buffalo Bill's show at the same time Mr. Witherspoon was and they had been great buddies until the show disbanded and Mr. Witherspoon decided that he was getting too old for such a violent way of life. Not so Uncle Sid. He promptly joined the Ringling Bros. Circus and for years drove the famous stage coach which careened around the big

121

top and in a final gesture of defiance burst into flames and gave oldsters as well as the youngsters a never-to-be-forgotten thrill.

In some idle time between acts he became enamored with a butterfly girl and married her and I think it was then that we lost tract of Uncle Sid. Her name was Edie and all I ever knew about her was that she hung by her teeth for hours on end until one day she let go and was a helpless cripple for the rest of her days. Uncle Sid then became an engineer on the romantic Canadian Pacific railroad and for ten years used the same tactics on engines that he had used on the horses. The company retired him at the age of sixty and he died a respectable man. However, I never forgave him for marrying the butterfly girl instead of Annie Oakley.

For Norm our sojourn in the White Mountains was really a vacation.

True, he hauled an unbelievable amount of water for us females to squander away, but nevertheless he was relieved of the strain of mentally calculating how many times the kids flushed the toilet at home or how many times the old Bendix went into convulsions.

The highlight of my time there was finding A. B. Frost pictures. One was framed and hung high in a gable up in the dorm. I found the other in the three-holer, and by that I don't mean a new Dynaflow. I could hardly believe my eyes, but sure enough it read, "A. B. Frost" so I boldly asked Uncle San if I might have them. He was most agreeable and in no time at all, I was the owner of two fine prints. I am now the owner of one fine print. Clint Ide took the one of a man shooting quail like a duck takes to water. Personally, I couldn't tell if they were crows or buzzards, but figured that Clint would get a great deal of pleasure out of the print. It couldn't have found a nicer home in which to be displayed. To us Clint and A. B. Frost will always be synonymous.

We left Punchy, alias the seven year itch, with my mother and journeyed on to Providence and Bonnet Shores. I have no fear that Howard McGrath's seaside establishment would have suffered any great financial loss if we hadn't paid our admission there for several days, but we tossed a few shackles his way and wondered why he hadn't harnessed the tide as yet. On our way back to New Hampshire we passed Walden Pond and Wade and I engaged in a little conversation about Thoreau, and Norm not to be outdone, asked, "Thoreau, who did he play football for?" so we relapsed into silence again.

Yankee Craftsmen and

No summer would be complete for us unless we visited our good friends the Sparks in Vermont at their partially disintegrated summer place. Margie had written me earlier in the summer that their ell had fallen away from the house proper and that they were trying frantically, but without result, to get one Doubleday, a Yankee Carpenter, to jack up the ell before it was too late.

Too late for what, I haven't as yet been able to determine. At seven o'clock on the morning we were to arrive, Doubleday and his helper arrived and proceeded to demolish the floor of the ell in lieu of starting the jacking up process. It was thus we found the Sparks family and Margie rushed out to greet us with "You would catch me with my ell down." Norm comforted her by saying he had seen girls in a worse predicament. I was so pleased to see Margie that it didn't occur to me to inquire when.

Margie had spent the summer papering and painting the first floor and it did look very cheerful and was definitely one of those shoestring decoration jobs that the house magazines love to depict. The bathroom was a very interesting room. It contained a medicine cabinet, a shelf full of Kleenex and a spinning wheel. I was thankful that I have always been possessed with a lively imagination and told Margie so. The bathroom proper was located at the far end of the ell which Doubleday was so busy tearing apart. Ray had pleaded with him earlier in the day to leave that section of the ell intact as the Smiths were on their way to partake of a bit of old Vermont hospitality. As the day wore on, the ell became further removed from the house until the point where it became downright alarming. At four-thirty, union time when Doubleday and his helper made ready to leave, not even the Olympic champion broad jumper could have made the jump from house to ell without doing himself bodily injury.

Margie, a real Scarlett O'Hara when it comes to putting off to tomorrow what could be done today, was not at all upset about the death leap. Mother came to the rescue and suggested that the carpenters run a gangplank from house to barn. It was no sooner said than done and we watched night fall without too much apprehension. Mother proved her superior intellect by not partaking of any liquids from four o'clock in the afternoon on, but Margie and I guzzled tea from dinner time on until eleven when we retired, and almost knocked each other off the gangplank in the wee small hours of the morning. Norm slept blissfully until five then started on the rounds to get the family organized and on the road. Wade was roused from his slumbering on the studio couch and Norm, who had not been too successful at getting us up, closed the studio couch with a terrific crash which succeeded in bringing our hostess flying down the stairs. She wandered around in a fog amid the aroma of burned bacon and coffee and hoped the Smiths would never, never come again.

By seven when Doubleday arrived we were packed, fed and ready to leave. Ray was out in his bathrobe shivering in the cold morning air and quietly cussing Norm out. The Sparks boys were sound asleep in their cots where they usually stayed until the unheard of hour of eight. Just as were to depart, Margie cajoled Mr. Doubleday into telling me a little ditty he had speedily told Margie the day before when they found an old cat hole between the barn and kitchen. In true Yankee fashion, he asked Margie why she didn't write it down so he wouldn't have to keep saying it. While Norm suffered a mild ulcer attack at having the early get away postponed, Mr. Doubleday gave out with the following:

"Sir Isaac Newton had three cats
A mother and her kittens
And in connection with the three
There's been a story written
And handed down to us as true
We give it in a rhyme to you.
These cats unlike most of their kind
Demanded much attention
When one would go, the other would

Which we need scarcely mention.
The trouble good Sir Isaac saw
Was so much scratching at his door
When he sat down to meditate
On one theme or another
His feline pets were sure to come
And put him to the bother
Of getting up to let them in
And oft he'd lose his subject clean.
At last a happy thought arrived
That would adjust the matter
'Twould please the cat and kittens too
Especially the latter
He made two holes, one large, one small
Through which his favorites might crawl
And now the great philosopher,
Intent on observation
Was to behold his wondrous plan
Put into operation
Through the large hole the old cat came
The kittens following through the same."

CHAPTER 4

WORLD WAR II

Phyllis wrote her mother, Ida Lee, at least two letters a week for many years. The following is just one of many newsy notes. Phyllis was 23 at the time.

Dear Mother,

I ask you frankly, does it every pay to plan things in advance in this crazy world? Poor Norm feels so badly about us having to postpone our visit to Kansas to meet that part of your family. I'll have to mail Lee's wedding gifts to her.

Mother, did I tell you that I am making slipcovers for the wing chair, and love seat and swages for over the windows? I'm going to start a hooked rug as well. I have a lot of pink and gray cloth.

Mother, Margie Sparks and I went to a fortune teller yesterday, and it was a most uncanny experience. She told me about Norm's sudden activation, and that you were a teacher, did creative work, but while not physically strong, were spiritually powerful. She said I had an older brother who was blonde, worked away from home, needed to be prodded, but was sweet and engaging. She told me I would have another husband, because my present one was a lot older. She said I would have my own sons someday, and they would be strong and smart. Encouraging? What I really want a nice little girl.

Try to come for Easter, and we'll go into Washington on the train. Your most welcome letter arrived last night and I really devoured it. Your weekend in New York must have been fun, but a bit chilly. I believe you enjoyed the fair. Aunt Stella and Uncle Sam are such gracious hosts for the Historical Society, steeped in knowledge of the folklore in that part of New Hampshire. Was Ken the drive on your last expedition? His new winter outfit sounds too snazzy! Does he wear that stylish hat?
Thanks for sending the picture of Frank's bride. She will be a hard task mistress, typical school teacher type… homely, poor soul.

Tonight we are hosting a buffet supper for twenty officers and their spouses. Norm suggested we have it here, and since the mess will cater it, no big problem. I am rather out of practice at getting ready for a large crowd. These are all wonderful guys who work for Norm, all fellow athletes, who were coaches as civilians.

Donnie is home today as it the Teacher's Institute. What a fine school. He has science and woodworking, both new to him. He eats lunch in the cafeteria, and plays on the seventh grade football team. He is still a baby though, timid about going upstairs alone.

Norma is getting along nicely at Seminary and doesn't seem to be feeling sorry for herself. She dresses well, plays sports and is still growing taller, making me feel small beside her. While she is somewhat boy crazy, she is too tall for her freshman classmates, and too young for the older boys.

Enclosed, find not one, but two pictures of my handsome husband. I must close and fix Donnie his lunch.

Love to you all, Phyllis

PS – I haven't told anyone, but you and Margie, that I am pregnant. Keep knitting for my baby. I have my heart set on a girl, but will plan to keep whatever I get.

Letter from Major Norman Wade Smith, USA, written from his station, Aberdeen Proving Grounds, in Maryland, to his mother, his mother-in-law by both marriages and his sister-in-law by his first marriage. As usual he used his trusty Remington, postmarked June 24, 1941. Bob was 15, Norma, 13 and Wade, 11.

Hello Everybody-Say, it is pretty hot down below the Mason-Dixon Line! Bob is with me and seems to like it. He is working at the post gas station, digging and planting shrubs and is black from the sun. He eats and sleeps at the officer's quarters. He is really quite big and is often taken as an officer. Bob finished first in his class all year, was elected to the Cum Laude Honor Society, and was the first freshman in school history to earn varsity letters in three sports.

Don is staying with his friend on a dairy farm. He takes care of chickens for room and board. They all go into the YMCA in Wilkes-Barre for a swim and a movie on Saturdays.

Sis is staying with Mrs. Altick, friends of ours in Trucksville. When Mr. Altick returns from a long business trip, Phyllis will return here.

We've rented a dandy place for $100 per month, but three couples will share. It is 11 miles from camp and is an old southern mansion named Thorn Meadows on 250 acres. The people who own it moved to Argentina, as he is a tobacco mogul, and she has a lot of money. The house is furnished. They want someone living in it, and thought is was their patriotic duty to rent it to Army officers. I sent Phyllis out to approve of the place, and of course she loved it. Don will live with us, as Bob and Sis will be boarding at Wyoming Seminary.

The place has a long driveway from the road with large pastures on each side. It has a huge terrace overlooking a swimming pool created from damming up a creek. The place is equipped with the most modern electrical appliances and has four fireplaces, and lots of crazy rooms with swanky furniture. We will be spoiled. It's like what you ready about or see in southern stores or movies. Please come and see for yourselves. The two other officers are married with one child each, and they work for me on our Special Services project. A farmer lives on the far side of the estate and takes care of the farm duties.

I guess we are lucky to find this place, especially since we've batted around so long in search of suitable living space.

Well, let us know how you all are.

Norman

Letter written by Phyllis to her brother, Ken, from Fort Deposit, Maryland, three days after the Japs bombed Pearl Harbor, December 1941.

Dear Ken,

You have been having a time of it haven't you? Sorry that you were so sick, but it is your fault for being so run down. Here are some stamps I came across. Are they any good? I wouldn't know a valuable stamp if it bit me on my nose! Well, what do you think of our being at war with Japan? They sure pulled a fast one on us. Too bad the USA wasn't better prepared. We are worried about Norm's brother, Cecil. He was back and forth from Pearl Harbor to Guam as a surveyor. Hope Grandma Smith hears that he is safe.

Norm and I were in Washington Sunday and it was so quiet and peaceful compared to the raging inferno it is today. Did you hear Roosevelt's speech? I had my ear glued to the radio since seven this morning in the den. Norm called me at noon, saying all Christmas and New Year leaves had been cancelled and his orders are to stand by for further instructions. Rumors of a transfer to the West Coast are popping up again. I can hardly wait for him to get home with the latest War Dept. Bulletin. Eleanor Roosevelt will be going to California to organize civilian defense. How I admire that woman. Well, it is my turn to get dinner, so I'd better be on my way. I've been too excited to think about food. Will keep you and Mother posted as to what happens to the Smiths. Tell Mother I plan to come home with the children anyway, if we are allowed to waste gas. Hope you are feeling better my boy!

Love, Pug

This letter was "written" by a 6 month old Punchy to his Dad in the Army, somewhere in Europe in November 1942. Phyllis' humor and gift for prose is evident in this ghostwriting job.

Dear Daddy,

Today I am 6 months old and weight 19 pounds and still look just like you. I like my family very much and they certainly like me. I can crawl now, so today Mommy bought me 2 pair of overalls. I also have a snowsuit, size 2, for these cold November days. I have a good appetite and eat everything Mommy puts on my plate. I haven't teeth yet, but I'm not worrying. My friends, Ellen and Rippy don't have any teeth either, and they can't crawl.

The other day a repairman from Sears and Roebuck was fixing the stove when Mommy brought me into the kitchen, and he said, "My God, look at those hands"! What's wrong with big hands Daddy? Mommy says yours are big too. I seem to be doing a good job of keeping Mommy out of mischief while you are away. I am a good boy all the time, and sleep from 6 to 6. I love our big German Shepherd police dog, but he keeps taking my graham crackers and fig newtons away from me when Mommy's back is turned.

We are getting ready for Thanksgiving, and maybe Grandma Oxley will visit. My big brother Bob will be home during the vacation. He scored a touchdown in the game against the Penn State freshman yesterday. I want to play football when I get bigger. Donnie and Sis are so nice to me Daddy. I am a lucky little man. Hurry up and get that war over with soon and come home to your newest son.

Love, Punchy

This letter was from Phyllis' brother, Ken, written from Italy, during the war. He came home to Cranston, RI, married Marge, had 4 sons, worked as truck driver, smoked good cigars, drank cold beer, drove Caddy's and was a wonderful brother. He would visit her frequently, parking his truck right next to Phyllis' house. She always worried what the neighbors thought. Ken died in 2006, after living his dream.

Dear Phyllis,

I received a v-mail from you today and am glad to hear from you. I guess you know you have been neglecting your old brother for a long time, but glad to hear from you just the same. I'm in the 94th Division of Patton's 3rd Army. Do you hear anything about us in the Army news? We spend most of our time maneuvering forward and digging foxholes. We know the Krauts are out there and we take a lot of fire, but not much up close as of yet. It's rough and often scary, but it will take a lot more than this to get me down. I'm okay mentally and physically, although some might question my sanity at times. I got the Combat Infantryman's Badge, and was put in for the Bronze Star for something that happened in an attack one day. I might get it, but then again, maybe not. All I really want is to get back to the states. I have a good German wristwatch and a P-38 Lugar pistol which I plan to bring home as mementos.

Give my regards to the family and Norm and the kids. Hope the baby is okay. Lucille is okay and plenty hardheaded. After the war, I'll know for sure. I write Mother every chance I get. I made her an allotment of $40 every month, and when I get my $10 for the combat badge, she'll get that too. I might even make PFC, but it takes some ass kissing, and that annoys me.

My views have changed plenty. All I want from life is a good job and a small home and a car, preferably a Cadillac. I don't want fame or fortune, not that it would come my way anyhow. No more questions or lines or red tape or Army crap for me. I'm going to burn my ties and hats, also. I plan to live like I want and do what I want, when I want to do it. I won't amount to a damn, but I'll be living life my way. I've done all the traveling and knocking around and high living I want.

My wild oats are sown and I'm turning over a new leaf. Do I sound like a preacher? We get plenty of wine and good cigars and cigarettes. I miss my Narragansett beer. Have eaten better here than in France or England, or even the states. Combat can be tough, but better than being a garrison soldier. No saluting or that kind of crap.

When you write to Mother, let her know you heard from me. How is Bob doing at Annapolis? Let Norm know where I am and my outfit. Haven't heard of the fellows you mention, but there a lot of us doggies over here. We are in the hills and it is very pretty, like New Hampshire or even Pennsylvania. The farms are run by old people and very young girls. It is getting late, so I'll close. Hoping this finds you all well, and happy.

Your loving brother,
    Ken

Chapter 5

CONNECTICUT SAGA

The Smith family relocated to northeastern Connecticut in the fall of 1950 to be closer to Phyllis' Mother Ida Lee, and Norm's Mother Flora Wade, both who lived within 45 minutes, to the east in Rhode Island. The Connecticut Saga articles covered numerous, humorous events from October 1950 through New Year's 1951, and were published in the Dallas Post, where Phyllis' Three Acres and Six Dependents were so popular. During this period Norm was still teaching and coaching at Wyoming Seminary, leaving Phyllis in charge of opening their new Connecticut farmhouse, and caring for Punchy and Keith. As far as the older kids, Bob was in the Marine Corps, Norma, awaiting basic training as an Army nurse, lived with Phyllis, and Wade attended the Coast Guard Academy, an hour south in New London. Norm's visit's were short, but action packed, as he cajoled numerous Yankee tradesmen in action, while personally living up to his own "handyman" moniker, "Bungle".

Unpacking In Woodstock

The McLean's wanted to move before the first of November, so we decided to move on Sunday, the twenty-ninth. We thought leaving a town on Sunday would be more discreet than moving into one. Norm was to see the vans loaded and I was to drive to Connecticut with Keith. Any one who has ever been in a car with the Smith brothers at the same time knows why I didn't add "and Punchy." I would rather pick up Malik, if he were hitchhiking than to be incarcerated in the station wagon with those two. They play a little game called "That's mine" from the starting point to the destination and it goes like this. Keith spots a tractor and says, "That's mine." Punchy promptly says, "No, it's mine" and the battle is on. After three hundred miles of that your temples are throbbing and you lose complete control and find yourself screaming. "Shut up, it's mine." I sought to avoid this very thing, so a pal of mine agreed to drive up the following day and bring Punchy, much to my relief.

We spent Sunday night with Norm's cousin and came up to the house first thing in the morning so as to be there when the vans arrived. Oh foolish girl. At five that night when Punchy and Evelyn arrived they found me sitting in the car looking very dejected. We knew the only thing to do was to drive on to Providence and spend the night with Mother. We did and came back early the next morning to find the vans had arrived the night before, so the men slept on the kitchen floor. One of the vans had broken down and delayed them. There were four moving men and I must say they had a great deal of patience with us. We had the big couch in two different rooms and then decided we wanted it back where we had it first, but they said very kindly, "No lady" when we made known our desire. One fellow had a patch over one eye and warned our kids never to play with firecrackers. He was the boy who lost an eye that way. He usually wore a glass one, but some fate had befallen it and he was waiting for a new one. Another fellow had long wavy hair which he felt inclined to run a comb through every so often and that held things up considerably. Of the others, one was very quiet and reserved and the other a friendly reminder that man hasn't been out of the trees for too long a time. This foursome combined with two fussy women who literally fainted every time the wallpaper and paint went right along with the furniture constituted a rough day. The men took the boys over to Putnam for lunch and brought us back hamburgers so we had strength to go on. About three-thirty, Mr. Comb decided they should leave. Evelyn overheard him say that "Under no circumstances will we unpack anything more", so we had to remind them that they were supposed to at least take back the barrels the dishes were in. They groaned and set a new world's record by un packing six barrels of dishes in forty-five minutes and not breaking one of them. At four they went driving off and we could see Mr. Comb in the cab getting his tresses in order for the long drive home. We made the beds, fashioned some sort of a dinner on the little two burner plate, put the boys to bed and literally collapsed.

We had forgotten the next night was Halloween and Evelyn was sitting on the floor in the guest room putting up her hair when we heard a loud explosion out front. I was in the bathroom putting up my hair, a rare thing for me, but the previous day had made me very hair conscious, and we couldn't figure out what had happened. I knew if it had been the oil burner we wouldn't still be upstairs wondering what the noise was. Just then another explosion rent the air and we could hear voices and a scrambling of feet outside, so we realized what was going on. Evelyn stayed until the end of the week and that night I had my first callers. It was a college classmate of Norm's and his wife and child. We were getting along famously until the oil burner started up and he remarked that they used coal as he felt so safe using it. That night I had trouble getting to sleep. I couldn't have been any less easy if I was waiting for old Vesuvius to blow its top. The boys were intrigued with the farm next door. Their association with the cows had been limited to helping drink up fifty dollars a month worth of milk, but now the very joy of being with cows was theirs.

Creativity In Cement

More than one night I have sat down to dinner with my eyes watering from the undeniable odor of barn. I like to see what I'm eating, so we have devised a bath before dinner routine. By six thirty they are in bed, but promptly at five the next morning the lights go on and the wrestling starts. To think I was concerned about not waking up in time to get the boys fed and off to school.

The first day we were here, Keith had dashed over to the farm and announced, "My name is Keith Smith and I want to be friends with your children." Rather a complete introduction wouldn't you say? Evidently they didn't object to the name, or the little fellow bearing it, as he spent the whole day over there. In fact, things were going to smoothly that I became a little suspicious. The next thing I knew Keith came home one night with his big brown eyes brimming with tears. I couldn't get any satisfaction out of him, so let him suffer unto himself until Punchy came home from doing his self imposed chores around the barn. Punchy came charging in like a Russian at a United Nations Meeting, and flayed Keith with accusations of ruining the cement on the barn floor. How one small boy wrought so much destruction was beyond my comprehension. I pieced together the whole crime. Keith had made imprints of his hands and feet in the lovely fresh cement and then as an afterthought signed his name with a stick to complete the picture. Naturally the two young farmers were unkindly disposed toward the young man who had ruined a full day's work. After dinner I hauled Keith over to apologize and he stood in their kitchen muttering all kinds of words not faintly resembling "I'm sorry" and we left. When we got in the car he looked up at me and asked, "Mom, what's apologize?" and I felt like one of those delinquent parents we have been reading so much about of late. Later that evening, I remembered what had caused

Keith's actions. Several years ago, Norm bought me one of those "whirl-around" clothes lines and was delighted to find the box which held it must be cemented down. This was right down the alley, so he threw together some of his super fast crumbling cement and went to work. As usual, he mixed too much of the potent stuff, so I ended up by having a large platform to stand on while hanging out clothes. The finished effect was breathtaking, so Norm assembled all available members of the family and had us put an imprint of one hand and foot in each corner of the platform. Punchy liked the ceremony, but Keith was a little tike and objected violently to having his bare foot pressed down into the cold slimy cement. It evidently impressed him because four years later when confronted by a cement job, he felt he had to leave his imprint there. I could see it was all Norm's fault that the kid regarded it as sort of a rural Grauman's theatre. That kid might go nuts in Hollywood.

Keith Takes Suffering To A New Level

A week after the day we moved in Keith developed a bad case of Pink Eye, and like most members of his sex knows how to suffer on a truly magnificent scale. He lay prostrate on a loveseat in the living room and ordered me to bring on the pinky, a battered blanket which has always been associated with collapsing from pain or fatigue onto a loveseat. He lay prone for about five minutes viewing the world thru rose colored eyeballs and then he staged a fast recovery and began to flit around the house and get all the toys he owns out. This went on till afternoon. I decided to have a bath and wash my hair (still conscious a week later) and then things began to happen. I had two phone calls. Keith answered the first one and told the operator who had a telegram for me that I couldn't come I was in the bath tub. I beat him to the phone, dripping, but triumphant to take the second call. I pranced back to the bathroom just as a large truck drove up in back of the house. There I was stranded. Keith rushed to the door and when asked if Mother was home said, "Yes, but she hasn't any clothes on." I called out for them to uncrate the stove and refrigerator outside and that I would be out in a few minutes. I bided my time and when the men were engaged outside I made a mad dash for upstairs. This house has several little architectural features that will bring tears to the eyes of my favorite architect, Donald F. Innes. The bathroom opens into the dining room which is something new in the field of floor planning I'm sure. I've heard of people who worried about baths at the head of stairwells. What if they had to contend with this. I intend to solve the problem by painting the walls the same color as the dining room, but Norm had an even simpler suggestion of just keeping the door closed. I told him that was automatically ruled out as you couldn't shut the door until it was re-hung or cut down to size.

He gave me his most debilitating "these dames who put charm before construction" look and I tried to wither sufficiently.

The stove is a thing of beauty. At night when it's all lit up you keep expecting the Long Island Railroad to crack up right in your kitchen. It has signal lights and warning bells and works so fast that it keeps burning things right behind my back. The refrigerator is too fat for the space allotted it, so we can open the door only part way. To remedy the situation we have to block off one door. If these situations keep arising, we won't have a door left to get out of the place.

After a full day of flitting around the house and getting in my hair, Keith developed an earache. When it got pink enough to match his eyes he started to yowl. Keith never cries or whines, he plain yowls. Sounds just like a coyote on the prairie with a full moon shining. He yowled me into calling the town doctor, a dear old man seventy-nine years old. He came promptly, and after a thorough examination of his ear, assured Keith he would live to see the sunrise the next morning. That kid hasn't missed a sunrise in six years of living.

The Boys And Church

During the week that Keith was home with the pink eye, the rector from the Episcopal Church came to call. He was very pleasant and included Keith in our conversation rather than ignore him. He asked Keith in all kindness, "How does your ear feel today little boy?" and Keith answered without the slightest hesitation, "It hurts like hell." Once the word was out and reverberating around the room he looked crestfallen and then with false courage repeated the word softly to himself a time or two and then said in loud tones, "That's alright to say. My Daddy says what the hell, every time we leave the wagon or bikes in front of the barn door." With that enlightened bit of information he settled down under the "pinky" and fell fast asleep. I should have told the rector what happened one never to be forgotten Sunday back home. Norm insisted that the boys attend church as well as Sunday school, and for Keith that was overdoing it. During the week he had picked up the phrase "shut up" and had been hard at work on it all week. How were we to know that he would try it out in church? He stood on the pew, listened to the minister for a second or two then said, "Shut up man." The man continued the sermon. Keith announced in louder tones the same words. We tried to hush him up, but the more we tried to hush the more insistent he became. He finally grew desperate and shouted, "Go home man", and with that Norm used a little "judo" and got him down on the seat. Just as it was time to rise and burst into song, we stood up and Keith made a quick getaway under the pew and when the hymn was finished we heard a voice saying, "I'm going now" and the door slammed. It slammed again a second later as Norm left to catch up with the offender, and administer some kind of punishment. When Punchy and I reached home, I asked Norm how he had chastised Keith and he said, "Are you kidding? When I saw him tearing down the road on those short fat legs

I couldn't help but laugh." From then on Norm and the boys went to church Sunday mornings and I stayed home. Norm claimed they never were naughty except when I was there, but knowing how prone Norm is to nap during the entire service I couldn't be too sure.

The boys seem to be enjoying their new Sunday school and I for one am looking forward to the Christmas program. Seems like Norm and I have been attending Christmas programs at church and schools all our lives. And to think before we get these two raised our granddaughter will no doubt be suffering through the same thing. Neither of us will ever forget Punchy's first appearance on the stage at Day School. He stood, like other Smiths before him, head and shoulders above the rest of the class. He was wearing short pants, a bow tie and pink ears plus a look of complete bewilderment. His mouth hung open and not a word came out, and no one in the audience mistook him for a quiz kid. Mr. Coughlin sat by me and he leaned over and asked, "Who's that big kid?" and for the life of me I couldn't say Punchy. Off stage he lost the grotesque look and I asked him why he didn't join in the singing and he said, "You should see how funny those people looked out there."

Slogans In The Cereal Box

By the time Norm gets here for Christmas, we may all greet him with a loud moo. This condition has been brought on by overindulging in shredded wheat. The boys laid in a supply the first time we went marketing and discovered that transfers of comic strip characters are included in each pack. So nice for Mother to iron on T-shirts when she hasn't anything else to do. Punchy, as usual, got the first transfer and was thrilled to have "Jug Head" pictured on his scrawny chest. Next was Keith's turn, and you should have seen his face when "Little Orphan Annie" fell into his cereal bowl. He is at the age where he can't imagine why girls are cluttering up this otherwise peaceful earth and then to have Little Orphan Annie come his way was almost more than he could bear. Punchy's good fortune continued, and he has a very good collection of characters gracing every available shirt. Every time Keith's turn comes around he gets Little Orphan Annie. At the last count he had six, but this morning something new came into his life. This transfer is about the dumbest thing I ever saw. It looks like something exploding and underneath it is written "Bam." Keith was so pleased to have the Annie chain broken, that he didn't stop to consider how silly he is going to look tearing around with "Bam" imprinted on his chest. I can see visions of his "bamming" off to school for a week at a time and his teacher wondering if he ever changed his shirt. I am sure the Orphan Annie shirts had her confused. We are all eagerly awaiting the "Snuffy Smith" transfer and I have every reason to believe Norm will find something in his Christmas stocking with that ironed on. Wonder how it would look on a tie? I can just see him flying around Seminary with a "Snuffy Smith" tie whipping in the breeze.

Turkeys Ride Greyhound

Since Norm has decided to "go Greyhound" I am praying for snow this Christmas. He has his route all mapped out and will leave the car in Kingston for Wade and have Wade go there and back by bus. The one thing that bothers me is Norm's idea of bringing nine turkeys home via Greyhound. I can see him now staggering onto a bus with his nine turkeys and all the passengers mumbling about these guys who wait until the last minute to do their Christmas shopping. I wonder if he's to bring the plow he's giving me for Christmas home on the bus, too? I better write to Bill and have him lock the turkeys in the freezer until Norm drives up at Easter time. I've heard folks say that a turkey tasted pretty good around Easter time anyway.

This should be a red letter Christmas for us. Santa has a choice of chimneys to alight in and we have enough room for a large tree. In fact, I'll be kind of sad if the tree doesn't topple over this year. The only year our tree hasn't is the year Norm nailed it to the floor, but I can't let him go to work on these floors. They're much too pretty.

Bunk Beds and Covered Wagons

This morning a most unusual event took place. Instead of being jolted out of the arms of Morpheus between five or six, I heard an anguished yowl from Punchy at quarter of seven. He was furious with himself for sleeping so late and was even more annoyed with Keith (the early bird I wish would get the worm) for being sound asleep. He yelled, "Wake up Keith. We've only got fifteen minutes to play (which interpreted means fight) until breakfast." Keith sprang out of bed equally provoked that he had overslept and the battle was on.

Yesterday they had started to play covered wagon with a vengeance. This game calls for the beds to be pushed together and everything they own piled on the beds. I had received instructions not to disturb the covered wagon, but Norma spent half the morning getting them organized, blissfully unaware that she was breaking up a trip into undiscovered territory. Since the room was picked up, we had prevailed upon the boys to wait until morning to start the trek west. Otherwise, the beds could never have been slept in. To get packed and underway in fifteen minutes was almost impossible, but the boys went to work like locusts in a wheat field and were soon underway.

A while later I heard Keith say, "Pretend it's morning and all the cowboys are getting dressed." Punchy was obviously annoyed, "Cowboys . . . listen, Fathead, we're pioneers." Fathead agreed to be a pioneer at any cost. For some unexplainable reason, Punchy had never gone all out for the Hopalong Cassidy trend. That coupled with the fact that we haven't television, practically assures me he will grow up to be a very difficult and maladjusted young man. The wagon started to roll and there followed much shooting and shouting at the mules. Then the obvious thing happened. Fathead was consumed by hunger. "Let's stop for breakfast," he suggested. Punchy said, "Let's wait until we get out of Indian Territory."

Keith was amazed at the size of the Indian Territory. He ventured softly, "Pretend you're married Punchy and your wife can fix our breakfast." "Married," Punchy yelled, "to a girl?" Keith said, "No, to a lady." Then a long discussion about girls, ladies, and how gruesome they all were followed. Finally, Keith said, "Bun's a girl." Punchy gave that a little thought then said, "Oh, no she isn't." Then "Oh yes she is, oh no she isn't" for a long time and then Keith announced with all the wisdom he could muster, "I know what she is. She's a mother." He had a good point there.

Before too much longer another heated discussion was under way. Whenever Keith defeats Punchy on some score, Punchy pulls off that old chestnut about things which occurred before Keith was born. Keith hates all references to events which preceded his birth. This time Punchy tried to convince Keith that the turkey run was constructed before his time. Keith remembers as vividly as anyone in the family, the great big stink about the building of the turkey run. Norm, to this day thinks it beautiful and well executed. Pretty soon Fathead, the pioneer, was in my room demanding justice. I said, "Punchy unfortunately we were all alive before that thing was thrown together." "Even Daddy," said Keith in a smug manner. Even Daddy was right. Without him and thirty-dollars worth of lumber plus two hundred and sixty pounds of misdirected energy, the turkey run would still be in the blueprint stage.

Phyllis and The PTA

Once the boys were in my room they forgot all about being pioneers and became what they really are, two itchy kids. Any Mother who can go through a full day without coming practically to blows with an eight-year-old boy is an angel in disguise. Our emotional bout starts at six every morning and lasts until bedtime at night. Punchy is constantly at war with himself and the world in general. He hates water, toothbrushes, casserole dishes and his Mother at times. All the intelligence he possesses is directed into one channel and that channel consists of disagreeing with me about everything.

Out of a clear blue sky Punchy asked, "Why don't you work at the school lunch program, all the mothers do?" It was the first I had heard about that, so I replied that no one had asked me yet. Punchy assured me that I would be asked and soon. It happened sooner than I thought possible. Soon after breakfast that morning, a nice woman came to call and brought me a lovely old dish which had belonged to the lady who used to live in our house. I knew the old adage of beware of Romans bearing gifts, but didn't realize what was happening until the woman was asking me to volunteer to help out at school one day the following week. I couldn't refuse.

Two nights later, I attended my first P.T.A. meeting. The president resigned as he was moving away and a woman I had mentally picked as a likely candidate for a friend was elected president. The school is a new consolidated school, very up to date, but like most schools overcrowded and the teachers underpaid. We were shown statistics about the number of students in school, the number soon to be in school, and it was frightening. The war babies of World War II were mostly responsible and before long the Cold War babies will be entering the public schools and there's no telling what the outcome will be. There followed a question and answer period, and I wish I had kept my big mouth closed. I simply asked why they hadn't built the school larger to start with. At that moment Mao Tsetung's proxy at Lake Success and I were enjoying about the same popularity. The hate waves came at me with supersonic speed and the place was in an uproar. The woman I had longed for as a friend glowered at me and said, "Shall we tell her why we didn't build a larger school?" It had all simmered down to the fact that they ran out of money. I wondered why they hadn't said so in the first place. That was something I could easily understand and the understanding was based on the experience of running out of money at the end of every month for the past fourteen years.

The P.T.A. meeting was a thing of the past, but I still had the school lunch program to look forward to. I fervently hoped I would fare better with food than I did with my fellow townsmen.

Picking Up Wade From The Academy

On Tuesday night before Thanksgiving the phone rang. It was one of those "will you accept the charge" numbers so I knew it was family, not foe calling. Sure enough, Wade's voice came bounding over the wires and after welcoming us to Connecticut on his own behalf suggested that the drive down to New London was unrivaled in beauty etc., which all boiled down to the fact that he had fifteen cents and his youth between him and a turkey dinner and would we please drive down to get him the next day.

Punchy came racing downstairs half pajamed to add his share to the phone bill and suggested to Wade that he get on the bus in New London, arrive in Putnam, and he would be there with his money to pay the bus driver. Wade was quite touched by the offer, but explained to Punchy that the bus people didn't do business that way.

The next afternoon found us at the main gate of the Coast Guard Academy waiting for Wade to come out. He brought a classmate with him who lived in Putnam so the boy said, so we started back home. It got dark early, but the friend seemed to know where we were going and showed us a few short cuts back to Putnam. When we drew near Putnam the friend explained that he didn't live in Putnam exactly, but near it. It is sort of like telling someone you lived in Paris just because you lived in France. We wove in and out of little roads the county had long forgotten about and ended up in Massachusetts. I told Paul he'd better call Wade the next day to plan their trip back, as I knew I would never be able to find his house again. I didn't want Paul to feel badly about having taken us out of our way, so I said, "You know I don't know my way around Putnam very well yet," and we parted on the very best of terms.

By then the little Smiths were ravenous and asking in loud tones, "When do we eat?" We gave the matter a little consideration and decided to stop somewhere for dinner. Wade thought it a wonderful idea, but wondered where five people could eat for fifteen cents. Norma, in a reckless and hungry moment confessed that she had money, so we found the most expensive spot in that section of Mass. and wandered in looking for all the world like Norma could afford it.

We couldn't have found a nicer place. There was television for the kids, bottled cheer for the adult, plus music and a cozy atmosphere. The kids mounted the bar stools with a grace which belied their having been raised in our kitchen in Huntsville, and we went on to order dinner. The boys joined us for dinner, but as soon as he had eaten Punchy vanished. It took Keith a little longer.

The Entrepreneurs

There is little of Henry the Eighth in that kid, inasmuch as he can't see leaving a bone around with any meat left on it. Since we all had lamb chops, it took him quite a while to get the table cleared. When our coffee arrived Keith left to see what the magic screen had to offer. Pretty soon Punchy came back grinning like a Jap, and showed us a handful of change. Wade remarked that he hadn't seen any slot machines and Punchy assured Wade that he never played the one-armed bandits.

He explained that he was taking men's coats and hanging them up as men came into the club and that he was being tipped for it. He dashed off and Wade looked helplessly at me and asked, "What are you going to do about it Mom?" and I answered, "Absolutely nothing." If any Smith in this outfit shows any inclination for making money, I'm going to fan it like a dying flame." Norma sighed, the sigh of people who work hard for their paycheck and said, "Punchy sure takes after Bob." I had realized that fact very plainly last summer. Keith at one time had possession of a broken carpenter's ruler and a dime. Punchy had sized up the situation so took the ruler away from Keith and climbed up on the terrace roof by way of ladder and left Keith yowling down below. Keith kept screaming for the ruler, so Punchy said, "Keith, I'll give you the ruler if you give me the dime," so the deal was , and Keith was pleased as could be for buying back his own ruler with his own dime.

I fear for that little lad's future. Punchy, like Bob, has nothing to fear. Bob had himself so many businesses while attending Seminary that I sometimes wondered how he avoided paying an income tax. He had a corner on the dry cleaning business and his usual morning greeting to classmates ran something like this, "Hey baggy pants where are you taking that boy?" or "That sure was good gravy we had last week" and if time permitted, he was known actually to help some protesting male out of his favorite sport coat and sprinted down to Marty's with it before the kid realized what had happened.

During midyears and summer prom time, Bob's income always took a skyward leap as he sold corsages for several florists. He sold more orchids than anything else then would show up at the dance with his date wearing something in the line of wilted sweet peas with much satin ribbon attached. It took all the self control the orchid buyers could muster not to trip him up, as Bob and the odor of sweet peas went wafting by.

All Bob's labors of love were passed on to Wade in sort of a package deal as Wade entered Seminary and much to Bob's disgust, only the semblance of a corsage business was left by June. Bob kept writing to Wade from the Naval Academy trying to inject a little money making spirit into his kid brother, but all was in vain. By June, Wade considered himself lucky to have sold enough corsages to get a small one for his date.

When we got ready to leave, we found Punchy still in business and Keith had fallen asleep while watching television and was propped up against the nearest drunk. Who was supporting who was a debatable subject, but we managed to get Keith down off the stool and headed for home. By asking questions and trying all roads, we found our way back home. It was one of those bright moonlight nights and the house stood out cold and formidable looking and Wade asked in an awed voice, "My God is that it?" and we had to confess that it was. After five minutes inside the house, Wade had discovered all the flaws it took me a month to find plus a few more. He stalked from room to room like a condemned man. Frank Lloyd Wright on a guided tour of Leavitttown couldn't have been any unhappier. He announced that we would be colder than the Artic in the winter (he can say that again) and asked in desperation where he could do any socializing. I assured him if things got too rough, he could go to stenciling class with me and with that he announced that he was tired and wanted to get into the sack. Norma and I collaborated and decided to give him the bed of which all four legs hit the floor at relatively the same time and that was all of the fault finding we were subjected to till the next day. On that day, Wade announced that the house wasn't entirely impossible and got out my typewriter and wrote to several friends and managed to convey to them the fact that his new home was a little east of Shanghai.

Storming Norman Takes Charge

Late Thanksgiving afternoon, we took Wade over to Putnam to meet Paul and they started back to the Academy. It was about the same time Norm and Evelyn would be leaving Seminary in the beat up Ford. I was excited as I would have been if Clark Gable were arriving by Cadillac that night. Norma and I thought they would be here about midnight, so Norma whipped up a cake for her Dad and we sat reading with an ear glued to the driveway for the sound of Norm's car.

About midnight I fell asleep and the next thing I knew it was two-thirty and I heard the car drive in. It had started to snow before they left Kingston and they thought they would never make it to Port Jervis. They went off the road entirely once and landed on a man's front lawn. It was little items like that which had made the trip a tortuous one. We got to bed just about the time the Smith brothers were getting up to start another day. Punchy said he would fix breakfast for himself and Keith, and I said all right.

I was awakened a few hours later by the sound of many feet racing up the narrow stairs and Keith led the triumphant assault into our bedroom. He had four boys with him and was pointing at our bed saying, "See I told you I had a father and there he is." The commotion aroused Norm and he opened one baggy eye and said, "Hasn't that dumb kid established his legitimacy yet? If he has, why don't they get out of here?" The gang departed and the Colonel went back to his snoring,

After breakfast, Norm started to check up on things and surmised that I had been here for over three weeks with my teeth in my mouth and nothing had been accomplished. I mumbled something about having a man come and measure for storm sash, but that I hadn't seen him since. Norm made out a list of things to do and after lunch was over, we started out to get things done.

Norm had been away from New England too long to realize you can't be a fireball around here. There are no unions in these parts. People work, when and if they have a mind to, and you just can't hurry any one up. I knew all this, but decided to let Norm buck the New England reticence that the Reader's Digest and Yankee Magazine love to depict.

Our first victim was the storm sash man, whom we found innocently at work in his shop. Norm charged in like Taurus the bull, and wanted to see the storm sash. See it? Heck, it had just been ordered the day before. When Norm recovered from that blow he made inquiry about the weather stripping around the doors. "What weather stripping?" He just couldn't shake the man's lethargy. Norm tried his most effective language. "Good night, there's so much space around those doors you could throw a cat out," then he added rather wistfully, "and we don't have a cat." Getting no response he consulted his list and item numbers. "We haven't any medicine cabinet in our bathroom," he announced. That item caused our friend no obvious concern. "Do you have medicine cabinets?" Norm inquired. "Yes" was his reply. We were making progress at last. "Is there any law against showing us one?" asked Norm, and the man brought forth the largest medicine cabinet I have ever laid eyes on. Norm, who judges everything by size, waxed ecstatic "Boy look at that Bun." I didn't say a word. "Don't you like it, Bun?" he asked and I said "Yes, but are you sure it isn't a small model Croxley Shelvador?" He got the connection and said, "That will be just dandy. We can keep extra coke in the bathroom," and he gave the man orders to put it aside with our name on it.

Our next stop was in Southbridge where Norm laid in a mountainous supply of bathroom fixtures. He had towel racks, soap dishes, glass and toothbrush holders, toilet paper holders, and an exaggerated opinion of himself as an installer of bathroom paraphernalia. He brought toggle bolts, new bits for his drill, a new hammer and screw driver and remarked that a workman was only as good as the tools he used.

On the way home the wind was blowing so hard, it was all we could do to keep the car on the road. The rain was coming down in torrents and when we reached home, Norma, who had been listening to the news, informed us that we were in for a tremendous storm. Forewarned is fore- armed, but we found that we could do nothing to keep the weather out. The rain streamed in through all the windows on the east side of the house. It came cascading down on my new wallpaper and before too long, we had pots and pans out catching the overflow and used every towel we owned to mop up the water.

Evelyn had planned to give me a Toni that night and announced that we weren't going to let any hurricane interfere. Norm and Norma took over the towel squeezing job while we started the hair curling job. I was all curled before the lights went out. The next day you couldn't tell which twin had the Toni, but you sure could tell the one who had been neutralized by candle light.

About five in the morning, the storm let up and we went to bed to get a little rest. Norm and Evelyn planned to leave about eleven Sunday morning and around eight Norm roused himself and I asked, "How did you sleep?" and he replied "Terrible, I dreamed I went shopping in my maiden form bra." "That's nothing" I said, "How would you actually like to go shopping in some Bauer and Black elastic stockings?" He thought the matter over and said, "Well Bun you're getting older and must expect some fleshy decay. I've got to get up and put up those fixtures for you now."

Right after breakfast, Norm started to work in the downstairs bathroom and by ten-thirty had only one large hole in the plaster to show for a morning's work. I asked him if he was fashioning a pass through between the bathroom and kitchen and he told me not to be ridiculous. I suggested it would make a wonderful gun site for Annie Oakley had she been born a few years later. He scoffed at that and then said in a very resigned tone of voice, "I guess I'm just not a plaster man. My best work is done on wood," and none of us had the heart to question it.

By eleven, Norm and Evelyn were ready to leave and I hated to see them go. Norm rolled down his window and reminded me to get on the ball and keep after the storm sash man and to get the doors weather stripped. In short, he wanted action before he came home for Christmas." What shall I do about the hole in the bathroom wall?" I asked, but by then the window was up and he was waving goodbye with the largest paw I have ever seen except on a Kodiak bear. I went inside and made up my mind to have the place all in order by Christmas, and a la Candide, you shall learn, "What befell a determined woman who thought to dress her home in storm sash and weather stripping."

Appliances Arrive

About an hour after John Barrymore Smith and Evelyn left, the pump began a mournful ditty. It chugged and churned itself into a rage, so I went downstairs to investigate, but Smith fashion couldn't tell a darn thing from looking. Both Norm and I come from a long line of people who look at but cannot repair things. I stayed in the cellar long enough for heredity to catch up with me, then came on up and called the nearest plumber, a man I must cultivate.

This man betrayed his whole profession by arriving promptly on a Sunday with all his tools. It didn't take him long to find out what was the matter. It was an unmistakable case of never missing the water till the well ran dry.

I considered in rapid succession murder (the man who told us the water supply was adequate), suicide (except I haven't picked out the third Mrs. Smith), so decided on a less violent course of action.

The milkman said he would be glad to bring us water in forty-gallon cans until the well filled. It was an admirable thought, but can you imagine sitting around waiting for a well to fill. I lack the Yankee patience. The plumber knew a well driller, so we contacted him and he promised to come December 22. Just in time for Christmas. Norm wanted action, so action he would have as well as noise.

On Monday, Norma and I hiked ourselves over to the Launderwell with our forty-eight soggy Turkish towels and did our share toward causing the biggest case of lint trap trouble the Launderwell had ever known. It did my heart good to see that everyone else had the same trouble. I was glad that we didn't have a television set when I saw all the aerials lying down, instead of looking skyward in hopes that Captain Video would drop in later on. There were a great many lost souls those few days following the big blow.

A few days later, I began to worry about our new deep freeze which had arrived in Conn. before we did. I knew we were paying storage on it, but couldn't seem to get hold of anyone with a truck. The freight office man called me one day, and I asked him to get in touch with a trucker and give me an estimate on having it hauled over to East Woodstock from Putnam. One man called and the price he gave me shattered me. I said, "I wanted you to bring it on a truck, not carry it over," and he snarled that the price would be the same. I said I'd call him back.

Meanwhile, a bit of good luck smiled on us. The washer arrived and both could be delivered at the same time, thus cutting down on the expense. They barely made it through the back door into the kitchen, and we could tell at a glance that the freezer would go through the narrow door leading to what we liked to call a utility room. It was really a refined woodshed, but since the utility room is highly thought of these days, we figured we might as well have one if in name only. The kitchen looked like a home appliance salesroom when the truckers left. You have all seen Alice in Philcoland, but a more devastating sight is Phyllis in Norge, Carrier, Whirlpooland. We seriously considered getting out the cloth poinsettias prior to Christmas and going into business. Lots of folks have a low appliance resistance around this time of year.

The Accidental Christmas Tree

While I was exhausting myself in the old familiar routine, Christmas kept getting closer and I still hadn't done any shopping. The house was hungry for greenery, and since we haven't anything resembling an evergreen on this small patch of earth, a trip to the woods was in order. I found myself remembering what had happened a year ago at Mad Acres. Punchy was the only kid in his room at Day School who hailed from the country. In fact, there was a strictly R.F.D. air about him which resulted in his being appointed a committee of one to bring in the greens to decorate the classroom. On arriving home from school, he made known to me the nature of his grave responsibility and I gave him permission to go out on the back hill and get into the spirit of the thing.

I had some friends there. We were all putting the finishing touches on our Christmas knitting, so Keith went along instead of me. The girls left about five-thirty and I meandered out to the kitchen to prepare chow and what I saw out of the window made me sick with terror. The boys had started out in obvious good spirits with all kinds of pruning shears and hatchets, but had been drawn to a lively little evergreen not more than twenty paces from the house, and had proceeded to cut it off at the ground and were busily sawing off it's little branches.

Norm had transplanted that tree the time we had our fire on the back hill and nurtured it along lovingly for four years or more. I simply could not believe a kid of mine would do such a dumb thing. It was one of those moments most parents experience at one time or another. You wonder why in heck all your good dominant genes had run off and left all the nasty little recessive ones to form a child who would cut down his father's favorite evergreen tree. Fortunately, Norm had faculty meeting that night, so wouldn't see the terrible mischief until the following morning. I couldn't bring myself to tell him when he came home, so went to bed feeling like a heel.

The next day came much too soon, and Norm hired himself to squeeze oranges and cook some of his loathsome hot cereal. He glanced out the back window and in the cool gray light of dawn saw something his eyes wouldn't believe. I heard him coming up the stairs, two at a time, and dove under the blankets and heard him roar, "Bun, do you know what those dumb kids did. They cut down my evergreen tree." He went roaring into the kid's bedroom bellowing with rage, but not a kid was in sight. Punchy had heard him coming up the stairs and he and Keith lit out for the comparative security of the guest room bed. He said later it was a good thing the kids had hidden or he might have really spanked them.

The ultimate result was that Punchy couldn't take the mangled tree to school, as Norm had done a taping job and hoped the tree would mend in time. To our knowledge Punchy hasn't cut down any more trees. In fact, he says the only evergreen trees he likes are Christmas trees and he didn't know how close he came to not having one last Christmas. Norm lost his Santa Claus spirit that year.

A Craftsman Finally Surfaces

About ten days before Christmas, I was down at the village store getting some meat out of the locker and at the same time talking a mile-a-minute telling the owner how frustrating it was to have a big deep freezer looming over you in the kitchen and not being able to use it. Later when I stopped to analyze all the activities that followed in the wake of that reasonably innocent remark, I think the man's first mistake lay in asking me why we couldn't use the deep freezer. I told him because we couldn't get it through the door into the back room, the old woodshed that was masquerading as a twentieth century utility room. After living here for several months, I am convinced it must have been the room they kept the corpse in until the spring thaw came and the grave could be dug.

Carl listened to my tale of woe and being a very kind hearted man brimming over with ye olde Christmas spirit which he keeps twelve months of the year, promised to come up that afternoon and see what could be done. I couldn't believe my ears, I hadn't seen the storm sash man since Thanksgiving, so this offer for immediate help out of a dilemma was more than I reckoned for. I hurried home with the good news only to be met by Punchy and Keith who were not at all interested in having a room for Mother to wash and dry and freeze in. Freeze in is right, without any assistance from the Carrier. That room was the great grandfather of all cold rooms I'm sure.

When we first came here, Norm's cousin had told us what a wonderful workman Carl was, but also said he is so busy all the time that we probably wouldn't have a prayer of getting him to do any carpentry work for us. Promptly after lunch Carl and two helpers arrived armed with hammers, crowbars, and a determination to get the job done promptly. They measured the deep freeze, then the door, shook their heads and went to work. I repaired to the living room with "The Cardinal" but even it couldn't compete with the music of hammers ringing and crowbars crunching. I was far more interested in the miracle being performed in the kitchen. I just love the sound of a hammer, provided of course that Norm isn't on the other end of it.

The kitchen drew me like a magnet so I put my book down and went out to see what progress had been made. They had crow barred their way down to the first fire that had blackened the woodshed and I saw bits of very old wallpaper here and there. I kept wising Nancy Warren was there to do something about it. Making sketches of old paper had never been in my line, but I understand that many of our lovely papers today came from just such beginnings.

The door looked so good with the sash off that I asked Carl if he wouldn't just keep on and make a large opening to sort of throw the two rooms into one and that is how the whole thing began. He looked a bit dubious, but I said Norm was used to such things as walls being removed, and never showed any apparent surprise when I decided a wall must be removed. As long as a wall wasn't needed to support something above, Norm never objected.

The opening looked gaunt and bare, so before long I suggested some scallops. The whole trend in building these days seems to be "when in doubt use scallops" so I suggested some to Carl and he agreed that the scallop was the thing, and as Frank Lloyd Wright said recently, we Americans deserve the architecture we have. My conscience was fairly clear though as we haven't a picture window which doesn't frame a picture, so I felt I could take a few scallops in my stride in spite of my tremendous admiration for the grand old man of architecture.

The simple afternoon's job was fast developing into a winter project. The room would have to be insulated, heated, painted and papered, new linoleum laid to match the kitchen not to mention the necessity of running hot and cold running water out there, so the washer could get into the act. I needed more cupboard space in the kitchen, so mentioned that to Carl and also suggested a breakfast bar for the morning rush hour. He scratched his head thoughtfully then turned to me and said, "In other words you want these two rooms done over," and I murmured faintly, "Yes."

That night when I wrote to Norm I had news for him. It began to look like we might get the freezer in the back room after all. We would have to wait until the linoleum was laid though, so I discouraged him about bringing home his nine turkeys on the bus. I told him to just bring one for Christmas then when he drove home at Easter time he could bring the others.

When Do You Stop Drilling?

The following Sunday, I went to church and when I came home found the big well driller being set up out by the back door. We weren't as lucky here as we were back in Huntsville. There they drilled right down into the old well and the water just had to be piped a few feet into the cellar. Here the well was half under the house, so drilling down that far was out of the question. They had to go around the well and all I could think of was how much copper piping it would take to reach the pump and storage tank at the other side of the house. The older we get, the unluckier we get it seems. It didn't help matters any to have the big boss regale me with the story of some poor man whose well was down two hundred and fifty feet and they hadn't struck water yet. At six dollars a foot you can figure out what a tragedy it was for those people. I said in a half joking manner, "If we don't strike water at a hundred feet we'll have to stop drilling," and he said, people hardly ever got water at that level. Especially us, I thought to myself. The big boss left and the two workers got busy. They arrived at the crack of dawn and worked until dark. Well drilling is darn hard work, but the profits must be good. In fact, you might call it making money hand over foot if you wanted to get corny about it.

In less than a week, the unbelievable happened. We found water, lots of water, six gallons a minute at ninety-three feet. People kept telling us how lucky we were. They didn't know that we thought we were living in a house which had an ample supply of water. Theoretically we had water. Now, all we needed was money, copper piping, a new jet pump, and a willing plumber.

Meeting Norm's Bus In Providence

Wade arrived home Thursday night before Christmas. He had a ride home with "Paul from Putnam" so we didn't have to meet him at the train. It was good to see him again and he tried his best to hide his disappointment at not being home in Huntsville for the holidays. However, he was full of plans for spending his vacation in Kingston. We broke open a bottle of rare old wine Wade brought home from his cruise and speculating on how the small Smiths might turn out. If they turn out to be half as nice as Bob or Wade, I'll be satisfied, but I have my moments of doubt. Sometimes I can visualize them in uniforms and by that I don't mean the clean blue of Annapolis or the Coast Guard Academy. I was thinking in terms of black stripes and perhaps the tinkle of ball and chain, if Norm moves the family to Florida.

What an age we are living in. Even Norm has a number now. If you aren't in the Army you have a social security number. It's all too much for my old non-mathematical bean. When Bob got out from Annapolis in the summer our clothes line was really a sight. You haven't seen a wash unless you've seen one with endless numbers of shirts and shorts all boldly numbered in black whipping in the summer breeze. Then along came Wade to add his number to the array and two summers ago an idle passerby would have gotten the impression that I was awarded the laundry concession from the Luzerne County Prison. Ah, memories, the very stuff that family life is made.

Friday we descended on Mother. The family who came for dinner, and stayed the night. Norm was to arrive in Providence at six-thirty Saturday morning and none of us had the character to start out from here on Saturday morning and be at the Greyhound terminal that early. The only solution was to get as far as Providence and then meet Norm early the next morning. Mother gave us a good dinner and then suggested that we go for a drive around town and see all the Christmas lights and decorations. Mother belongs to the era which considers a car something to go for a drive in. I don't know of anyone who just goes for a drive, except Mother and her contemporaries. A car to us is a way of getting from one spot to another out of necessity, and nothing more.

It was a cold, icy night, but we went for our drive and after touring down town Providence, we decided to call on my brother and see his new little son. Mother thought it would be nice for our boys to see their little cousins and tree. We saw the cousins, but the tree wasn't there. Ken was to bring it home that night. About an hour later Ken arrived treeless smelling more like Four Roses than a hemlock bough. He just forgot the tree, he declared. His wife thought they were the only ones who didn't have a tree. Ken said not to get morbid about it, he'd get one tomorrow. I asked

Ken, who is a prolific reader, if he hadn't been reading all the warnings about the foolishness of office parties and he said, "Listen to the girl. So I drive a trailer truck and she thinks I go to office parties. What do you think I am a white collar worker? When Truman gets through with me in March, I won't even have a shirt." I figured he had exhausted about three of the four roses in that blast, but he still had the fourth one to toss. "Things are getting so tough down there that next year we'll be under the trucks draining the anti-freeze for a little Christmas cheer." Suddenly he became the man of the house. He sprang from his feet demanding his dinner and a look at his new son both in the same breath. He tripped over the electric train the playful little cousins had spread out all over the dining room floor and fell flat on his face. It was as good as a Charlie Chaplin comedy any day.

Mother had long since given up trying to keep things on a high intellectual plane. In falling, Ken had disconnected the A.C. wires from the control box. Punchy tried vainly to repair the damage, but couldn't, so asked the last man in the world whom he should have asked what A.C. meant and where the wires went. Ken said he didn't know and didn't care, but Punchy kept asking anyway. Suddenly a ray of knowledge found its way into Ken's brain and he said quietly to Punchy, "A.C. means "After Christ" and it doesn't have anything to do with a train," and after imparting that great bit of information made for the kitchen and his dinner.

When the cousins started to bang each other on the head with the trains, instead of letting them run on the tracks, we decided it was time to go. Time to go home, well not directly, a little side trip to Roger Williams Park was in order. Seems like everybody else in that large city had the same idea, so we just followed the crowd. The park does have a beautiful display every year and I consoled Wade who was driving, by telling him that we used to take him to see the display there when he was a little boy like Punchy. "Like Punchy?" he asked in a scared voice and we had to laugh. In fact, we had come across an old snap shot of Wade and one of the donkeys in the manger scene and Punchy was quite intrigued by it. He hastened to tell Wade about it and Wade asked Punchy how he knew it was him, and Punchy fortunately has inherited Norm's wit said, "You were the one with the hat on." Evidently having the engine of the electric train banged on his head once or twice earlier in the evening hadn't slowed him down any.

Soon, we were back at Mother's cozy little red house and after having some cocoa and cookies put the boys to bed "temporarily" to quote Mother who knew darn well they would be racing around by six in the morning. We all felt it was too bad they couldn't drive as they would be the ideal ones to meet their father on the six-thirty bus. Wade said he would get up with the boys and take them down with him to meet their Dad. Norm is a little like the father in "Cheaper by the Dozen." He likes to line up his boys up and look them over while they stand at attention. He says the only thing he doesn't like is the long time between sons, but he can't blame that on me.

The living alarm clocks went off a little before six and routed Wade out of his bed and the three sons were off to meet their father.

Where Is The Colonel's Luggage

I had our day all planned, but as usual things didn't work out the way I thought they would. Right after having breakfast at Mother's, I thought we would leave for Connecticut. We didn't have our tree or any decorating done and the boys had a Sunday school program to appear in that evening, so I was anxious to get on home. I told Norm my plans for the day and he agreed except for the immediate departure for home. His luggage had not arrived with him and he was to meet the next New York bus on which his bags should be. We were just innocent enough to think they would be too, so we said goodbye to Mother and drove down to the station. The bus was there, but no barracks bags belonging to our hero. We were assured that the bags would be on the next bus which was due to arrive two hours later. I suggested calling on some relatives, so we did, then met the next bus. No bags. The strain was beginning to tell on the Colonel. He muttered something about going through World War II with far more baggage and not losing it anywhere along the line. Until three that afternoon we called on friends, relatives, and met every New York bus, and we ran out of both patience and relatives at about the same time. By then Norm's ulcers were really all stirred up. He wasn't worried about his personal belongings, but he had wrapped a turkey in a white shirt and was bringing it home for our Christmas dinner. I decided we couldn't wait around any longer, so Norm arranged for his bags to be put on the Putnam bus, when and if they ever reached Providence. By that time he had every one in the bus terminal worrying about his gear and one poor man asked him not to make such a stink about it and Norm replied, "If you think I'm making a stink, just wait a couple of days and you'll see what a stink is really like."

Storm Sash and Christmas Trees

The kids were fussy on the way home, so Norma a child psychologist if I ever knew one, suggested a new version of the old word game. The one who was "It" gave the initial or initials of something pertaining to our family in connection with Christmas, or just pertaining to Christmas. For example, C.D., any fool knows that means Christmas Decorations. I made the mistake of guessing something correctly so I was it. I thought of a lulu. It was P.P. (Punchy's Presents) and it had everybody stopped. Norm had been quiet. In fact, Wade was driving and Norm was enjoying a little turkey-less snooze in the back seat. The kids wanted him to play the game with us. We gave him the initials. "Purple pickles," was his quick response and Wade said, "You can see Dad has food on his mind."

All the Christmas tree stands we had seen the day before had vanished into thin air, so we arrived home treeless. I kept waiting for Norm to ask about the storm sash, but he didn't mention it until we were driving up the driveway. He glanced out the window and made a startling observation. "There's nothing objectionable about the storm sash, Bun. In fact, you can't even notice it." Punchy asked, "What storm sash" and with that Norm took another look and said, "Goodnight isn't that on yet?" and I had to admit it wasn't. Then the third degree questioning started. What did the man have to say? Why wasn't the storm sash on? Why didn't I call the man and say cancel the order, we'd get some somewhere else. I knew when to keep quiet and I did all the while Norm was eyeing me with a special look he has for me when he thinks I have been vegetating instead of producing. I assured him that now he was home, he could get busy on the phone and get things done. He thought if anything was to be done he'd have to get busy on the phone. It was then he broke the devastating news that he was planning to insulate the attic while he was home. I wanted desperately to be a good sport about it so said, "O.K. Johns-Manville, it's all yours."

The boys went down to the Post Office for the mail and the store keeper was so upset to hear we didn't have a Christmas tree that he literally wrapped one around Wade's neck. It was a small, well shaped tree, unlike anything we have ever had before. We put it upstairs in the playroom and the kids got busy and decorated it. Meanwhile, Norm divided his time between the phone and the electric candles. I came downstairs once to check up and found the phone on a window sill, and a candle on the phone stand, so I suggested he finish one job and not try to mix the two.

We had dinner and went to the Sunday school program. We had a hard job convincing Norm to go. He wanted to sit all alone by the telephone feeling blue about his turkey, but we insisted he go to church with us. After the program we went to a cocoa party (how my life has changed) and then home. Wade had stayed home to answer the phone, but he hadn't had to move all evening. Norm was really beside himself. The last bus for Putnam had arrived and his bags weren't on it. He called Providence, New York then Putnam again. We all had to be very quiet as Norm can't hear very well on the phone. He was really mad at the Greyhound Company. Pretty soon we heard him say, "I want to talk to the big hound," and Wade said, "We better do something to distract him Mom." He told us later he had asked to speak to the big boss and wouldn't believe us when we told him he asked for the big hound. The man in the Providence terminal assured Norm they had sent a tracer out and that everything possible was being done to locate the lost baggage.

"Tracer," Norm roared, "Get some bloodhounds on the trail. Do something man," and wished him a Merry Christmas. We still had Sunday to look forward to and Norm resolved he'd have that turkey by Christmas Eve or else.

Digging The Cellar

A loud pounding on the back door brought us down from the attic. One of the workers had come to help Norm dig down to the cellar floor level, so the new pump could be installed. The finishing touches on the attic would have to be left until Norm's next trip home. He was to bring a small hand stapler and staple the saggy parts together. The job shouldn't take more than five years at the most and quite a few staples, so we have that to look forward to.

It was a cold windy day, but the two men started digging a hole around the big pipe which stuck above ground level. It was supposed to have been removed by the well men, but no matter what they did they couldn't disengage it. The idea of leaving the pipe behind had caused Mr. Goldberg no end of distress, but a new well drilling job reared its ugly head so men and equipment had left our premises. By the middle of the afternoon the diggers had dug down to a level with the eight inch pipe and I swear Mr. Goldberg must have had a carrier pigeon cruising about overhead. It was positively uncanny the way he arrived in time to remove the big pipe in five minutes after it had been uncovered. Norm said later that from the expression on his face, he couldn't have been happier if they came across some uranium. We agreed that sometimes it doesn't take much to make people happy and we took to wondering what form ours was going to take some day.

The excavation was very interesting to watch. When the assistant was down in it, you would think the job was about finished, but then the Colonel would step down in and much of him was still above ground, so they would go on digging. Norm is a hound for any hard physical labor and the poor man helping him said later that he thought Norm was never going to stop digging, I told him about Norm working behind the tractor back home when we excavated for the terrace. The man he helped then was famous for hard work, but just the same, Norm almost finished him off. Norm's job was to hold the scoop behind the tractor and then dump it at a certain point. Usually on a job like that the earth made the scoop so heavy that Walter was used to jumping down off the tractor seat and helping his helper dump the load. Not so with Norm. He managed to heave the scoop up in the air and empty it before Walter could turn around. They worked together like a pair of faithful mules and one day they unearthed a horseshoe. "Whoa," roared Norm to Walter, "I lost my shoe." Walter turned around in time to see Norm holding the horse shoe up to the sole of his number twelve army boots and he had a good laugh about that.

At the end of a week, you would have thought that Norm had spent his entire life behind a tractor. The two men worked together in perfect unison. In fact, they even got to the point when I was suspicious that they were showing off a bit for my benefit. I didn't like the way they went down the front bank almost to the fence and then turned around as only a tractor can turn on the proverbial dime. I warned them to watch out for the fence, but they paid no heed. One afternoon I heard a splintering noise, but didn't connect it with the fence in particular. A few minutes later, Norm was in the laundry arming him with a large roll of adhesive tape. That in itself should have caused me to become suspicious, but I was enjoying one of my "more faith in human nature days" and didn't pay any attention. When I went down for the mail, I saw the terrible mischief and hastened up to complain about the fence to them. I said my little piece and then Walter looked at Norm and said, "Isn't that just like a woman. We would have been killed had we gone over the stone wall, but all she cares about is the fence". At that moment he was so right. I had helped to build that fence one day when the thermometer registered 103 in the shade and it meant a lot to me. It was one thing around the place that hadn't been taped together, so you can appreciate how I felt.

Keith and The Steamroller

A similar thing had had happened the Christmas Keith was two. We had bought him a steam roller and he was merrily riding along the upstairs hall, but came too close to the top step so both came crashing down the stairs. I ran in to see how much damage the new paint job had suffered, Norm estimated the damages to the steam roller and then Mother with a voice edging on sarcasm asked if anyone was concerned about the child. Keith had disentangled himself from the crash and was giving vent to loud cries, so we knew he was alright. In fact, we are more or less Spartans about the kids in some ways. Too much sympathy brings on many more tears and if you just go on as though nothing happened, you can usually convince the kids that nothing has. Five minutes later, Keith had forgotten he had fallen down the stairs and was merrily chipping fresh paint in the living room. I wondered in what mad moment I had fallen for the steam roller anyway. In Robbins and Uhl it looked good, but in the Smith house it was a force to be reckoned with. Naturally it proved to be the only toy that took Keith's fancy and I am sorry to say it lead a long and destructive life. I was glad when spring came and we could relegate it to the great outdoors.

By nightfall the hole was down on a level with the cellar floor. The assistant crawled over to his truck and departed, but Norm seemed none the worse for wear. His wonderful shirt had kept him warm and he was more than pleased with the progress he was making. He had made arrangements to have the doors weather stripped the next day. Mr. Stormsash had made no move along that line and besides we had long since lost faith in him, although he had actually called Norm the night before to announce that he had located some windows somewhere. They were new and would have to be painted, but if everything went well, we should have them on by pussy willow time. He wanted a check for such and such an amount, so Norm wrote one and he said he would stop by for it whenever he happened to drive by. No reckless man about using gas was he.

Church and Christmas Eve

That fearful and wonderful day known as the day before Christmas arrived in due time, and by nine o'clock the Battle of the Baggage or the cold war between Smith versus Greyhound was in full sway. The turkey was by then worth its weight and then some in phone calls, but Sherlock Smith was determined to have his turkey for Christmas dinner or else. Our phone did ring once and one small Smith was almost trampled to death by Norm as he rushed to the phone only to find out it was the wrong number.

Norm and I were busy in the kitchen and Wade kept the boys amused and it was lunch time before we realized it. After lunch, Norm told us to go ahead and make the filling and all of us had the presence of mind to question the orders. If he wanted to pretend he was going to have a turkey dinner the next day we decided to let him. I asked Norm for something I knew was out in the barn, so we got him out of the house for a little while.

Punchy was in a tizzy to decide which church program to go to that night. Since we moved here he has been going to two churches each Sunday and when we think back on how he used to fuss about going to one, we wonder whatever has come over him.

Norm couldn't believe it when he heard Punchy trying to make up his mind about which church to go to Christmas Eve. He remarked, "If this keeps up Bun, he'll be ready for Yale Divinity come fall." No such momentous decision was confronting little Fathead. He was going to be a good Episcopalian that night and go to his own church. Besides, he had the inside dope that Santa would be at that church and that was where he was going. Fathead's night life has been very sketchy, so he was put to bed right after lunch so as to be in condition to meet Santa that night. If Santa only knew he was going to meet Keith I think he would have taken a nap too.

With Norm out in the barn and Keith napping the house was very quiet. At the local church program, Punchy and his cohorts were to wear choir robes and sing; so in true man fashion the uniform won out. The only thing an eight-year-old boy can look angelic in, except his sleep is a choir robe. We had hauled the suit over to the Laundromat the previous week and had the white surplice starched and ironed. At four o'clock Punchy sighed and told us of his decision and then as if to really convince me he said, "Do you think I want you doing all that washing and ironing for nothing." I was tempted to say I had been doing it for nothing for fourteen years, but decided what's the use? When we first were married, Norm used to give me a dollar each wash day for pin money, but when I finally got wise and did a wash every day, he quit being so generous, so I went back to the old weekly routine.

On Christmas Eve we old folks sat around the living room fireplace like a bunch of draft dodgers and wondered when the boys would be home. Norm remarked that times had certainly changed since he was a boy. He used to stay home on Christmas Eve, but there we were old enough to go out, but sat home while an eight-year-old boy and a six-year-old boy went in opposite directions to celebrate Christmas Eve. It was certainly not the way all the magazines had depicted home life.

The Luggage Arrives

At nine o'clock the baggage arrived in Putnam and we were informed by way of phone. They offered to send it over by taxi but Norm said no they might get lost on the way to our house. Wade and Norma drove over in the station wagon to escort the bird home and Norm was like a kid when they got back, and he found the turkey safe within his white shirt right where he had put it. It smelled all right, so we stuffed it and had it already to pop in the oven early the next morning. It was eleven o'clock before we got the boys to bed and then we had to start getting ready for their Christmas. Norma kept saying, "What would we be doing if we didn't have the boys?" and the Colonel grumbled that he would have been in bed hours ago. He and Wade had a terrible struggle getting the new electric train set up. Neither is mechanically bent, and I thought that they would never get it to running. During the war years when Wade was my right hand man about the house, I used to get so provoked that he could never fix anything for me. He had a stock reply for anything that needed fixing and that was, "It'll have to be welded." To this day, if any one mentions welding I get annoyed. Think I'll give Wade a portable welding outfit when he gets married then he can be little Mr. Fixit around his own home. Punchy said something about welding to me the other day and I asked him not to say that word around me and he asked, "Why is it a swear word?" and I replied, "No worse than that," then went on to tell him about Wade and his mania for welding.

Opening The Stockings

Norma had all kinds of nice things for the boys' stockings. Every year she puts a silver dollar in the toe as well as the traditional tangerine and nigger toe nut. The stockings were too heavy to hang on the mantle without being nailed, so we pinned them to the foot of the boys' beds. By two o'clock all was in readiness so we retired for a short nap. At four I heard Keith out in the play room crying because Santa had taken his stocking away. Punchy woke up and discovered his within reach so told Keith to get back in bed and open his stocking, The remarks were priceless and I will never forget Keith's awe inspired voice saying, "Gees Punchy, look at the big nickel." He might not be too far off either as you get about a nickel's worth these days for fifty cents. You can see what inflation has done to that young child already. At four-fifteen the first shrill blasts of the Super Chief assaulted the Colonel's sleep and he said, "We might as well get up Bun," and we did.

At Last Christmas

We got through Christmas Day somehow. Dinner was rather rushed as Wade was to leave Putnam soon after twelve to start his trip to Wilkes-Barre. The turkey was beautiful to behold and the Colonel remarked that it didn't taste doggy at all in spite of a long drawn out friendship with a Greyhound.

Once Wade departed the remnants of the almost extinct Oxley family arrived and we had a great old family get together. Ken had finally caught up with a Christmas tree somewhere in or around the city of Providence, so was once again in solid as a family man. The cousins spent the entire afternoon feeding the electric train pills which caused it to belch forth smoke, and making it whistle loudly most of the time. The tragedy of the afternoon was when our company left and Norm instigated the much hated pickup time and little Fathead discovered that his "big" nickel was gone. We did more damage looking for the silver dollar than the kids had done all afternoon in the playroom. Bedtime came very early for all that night as Norm was anxious to get up early Tuesday morning and start a minor revolution around the house.

Getting Some Work Done

Promptly at six the next morning, Norm leaped out of bed and mentioned that some pancakes would be just the thing to start off the day. I agreed, but showed no indication to do anything concrete about it which annoyed him no end. He started to ask me what kind of flour did I used, did I put any eggs in the mixture, and wouldn't it be easier to get up and make them myself instead of telling him how to fix them. I agreed and by then the boys, who had undoubtedly heard mention of food charged into our room and were told by their Dad that "Bunny girl" just couldn't wait to get up to make pancakes for them. It was beginning to sound like a soap opera and not a very good one at that, so Portia Smith stepped forth from bed and faced life for the thirteenth year in this drama of everyday life of which we are all more or less responsible.

While I did the breakfast dishes, Norm called the few people he knows around these parts and then he called quite a few people he didn't know. Mr. Stormsash was contacted but with no marked success. He couldn't get any storm sash for us he said, but had neglected to call and mention the fact. One special ulcer Norm has set aside for lack of storm windows started to act up, so he asked old Stormsash to get some windows and get them on while he was here to see that the job was done. On the phone it all sounded very simple and logical. It was going to be a long winter, but storm windows plus the insulation of the attic was to help bring down the oil bill which by that early date was something to be reckoned with. If you want less heat for more money I know the answer.

By nine all able bodied workmen had been contacted, so Norm and the boys took off for Putnam leaving me to greet carpenters, plumbers, two linoleum men and one hopeful insurance man whom we hadn't called. He must have just followed the traffic and ended up in our back yard. Fortunately in his case, Norm was several miles away as he has no insurance resistance whatsoever.

We had a nice little social gathering, strictly non union, no portal to portal pay to louse up the morning. Just good honest people willing to work, but waiting to see what the big boss wanted done first. The plumber was a large, good hearted man whose job was to run some heat out to the woodshed, also hot and cold water for the washer, put the jet pump in and then hope he could collect for the job. The carpenters who had been here for a couple of weeks were willing to go on adding scallops indefinitely, but agreed to take time out to fix a shelter for the new well in the cellar and do any odd jobs that Norm wanted done. The linoleum men departed saying they would return the next day and then Norm came home with a station wagon full of insulation bats and energy to match the amount of work to be accomplished in the next few days.

The plumber stayed until we got into a heated argument about how to keep the soon to be installed pipes from freezing. Mr. Copper suggested an electric cable to be wrapped around the pipes beneath the floor.

Nothing could have agitated Norm more. He is the most violently anti-electric person I know. He nearly hit the ceiling when the words electric cable were mentioned. One redeeming feature of this place is that the meter box is in a remote corner of the cellar where it doesn't call attention to itself. In Huntsville, the clear round glass box was in plain view and caused Norm no end of distress. On many a bright summer day, we have seen him careen around the corner behind his power mower, stop and peer at the glass disc and if some sneaky old appliance was on and the needle was telling on it, Norm would stop the mower, creep cautiously into the kitchen and sneak up to all things created of white porcelain with bent ear and hatred in his heart. We caught him in the act one day and from then on he was called old Killer Kilowatt and he didn't know why he claimed.

After lunch Norm said he would get into his work clothes and start the attic job. He owns several interesting sweatshirts which he acquired during a hitch in World War Two. These shirts are impregnated with some vile smelling chemical and were to be worn in case of a gas attack. Fortunately, he suffered no such an attack, so the shirts came forth when some very special project is to be attacked. I might add the shirts are never hard to locate in the attic. Even with moving, that compelling odor led Norm straight to them and I was hopeful that they had been misplaced. When Norm came downstairs trailed by the heavy smell of chemical warfare with feet shod in the combat boots, Punchy was truly impressed and thought that things would really hum around here that afternoon. Smart boy ……

Copper Pipes and Weatherstripping

Norm had bought anti-electric cable to keep the laundry pipes from freezing from the very start, so Mr. Copper Piping and I agreed to run the two radiator pipes and the two water pipes along the baseboard. I was more than anxious to get my washer hitched up and the plumber was more than anxious to finish up his work here. All the while he worked here he kept shaking his head and warning us that we were going to an awful lot of expense which didn't help our morale or our diminishing bank account the least little bit. He reminded us constantly how fortunate we were to get copper piping. At roughly a dollar a foot, I failed to see where the fortunate part came in, but I was polite and nodded my head at the proper moments.

I wouldn't go so far as to say that the pipes were inconspicuous, but at least they were thin and defiant looking and the kitchen looked more like a subway every minute as the day wore on. Norm said he hoped Orson Welles wouldn't drop in and when the plumber asked him why, he replied, "Well you know what he did for the sewers. This might prove quite inspiring." Evidently, Mr. Copper Piping didn't waste his time at the movies, so it was lost on him, but I giggled in an appreciative manner but not loudly enough to encourage Norm. He never has recovered from that long chase below ground and every time he spies a manhole cover, he suggests that I drop in and then he'll chase me. I should be safe forever in this town, but don't know that I'd trust Norm in New York.

Meanwhile, work in the cellar was progressing. The well pipe opening had been surrounded by three walls of concrete blocks carefully mortared together. It was a work of love, and much too fine I thought just to surround a well pipe, but then I didn't know. Some friends of ours had to pull their pipes once and had to remove part of the roof to do it, so we were profiting by their experience. I hope I never live to see the day these lovely copper pipes have to be pulled. However, we now have what I believe to be the only bomb shelter in this small town. It may take an atomic attack for me to become popular around here. So far my Hooper rating is low, low. However, my atomic bomb morale is high, high, high. You can't have everything.

It was four below zero that day and even our rugged carpenter friends, who had weathered many a cold Connecticut winters, were forced to admit it was a bit on the chilly side. They had three doors to weather strip, so they erected a little wind break to keep from freezing to death and one by one the doors were yanked off, the wind break erected, and the weather stripping done. The oil burner and I both protested loudly all the time and of the two, it would be safe to say I gave off the most steam. The competition was definitely not keen, just expensive.

Black Door Locks

Work was progressing so favorably then that Norm decided a trip to town was in order. The fact that none of the doors had locks bothered my mother and besides the back door was not adverse to blowing open in a high wind and staying open until discovered by someone. We decided to invest in an attractive looking, black wrought iron handle and lock so the door could be locked against the wind and whatever dangers Mother had in mind. I guess city dwellers just aren't of a trusting nature as country folk. We never locked the doors at Huntsville unless we went on a trip somewhere. One night Wade locked us out and we aroused most of Huntsville before we got him awake. His window was open and we threw snowballs in until he became saturated with cold wet snow and realized something unusual was going on at that hour of the morning. The Lord and master proclaimed that from then on the back door was to be locked only when he saw fit. The proclamation was delivered in loud enough tones to awaken the small boys who were always anxious to start a new day. In fact, the whole family had come to life, so I gave up and went down and made pancakes and thought longingly of sleep. From then on, the key was either, lost, bent or broken so caused no more family friction. Wonder what Sis and Bill are using for a key these days?

The lock Norm found was very good looking but was brass was on the inside. You would have thought my word was law. He told the salesman he liked it, but I had ordered a black one. The salesman then conceived the bright plan of painting the brass part black. He was anxious to make the sale and Norm was anxious to get the back door locked. As for me, I wished they'd left it the way it was black wrought iron on the outside, brass on the inside. The hardware store Picasso went to work immediately and Norm promised to return for the lock first

185

thing in the morning. I didn't dare tell Norm I loved brass when he told me the brave and courageous thing Picasso was then engaged in doing. I knew the black paint would wear off in no time as all the Smiths are given to going in and out of doors a great deal more than most folks. In fact, they almost knock each other down at times in passing, so I knew the paint job wouldn't last long. If worse came to worse, I could get busy with some paint remover and have a brass knob eventually.

Norm brought the lock home in great triumph and showed it to the men who were to install it. They admired it and said they would go to work on it after lunch. Norm, who has mania for neatness gathered up the paper the lock had been wrapped in and threw it into the dining room fireplace which we kept roaring most of the time. Neatness at times is a virtue, but at this time it proved to be a nuisance. In the papers were the little black screws which were needed to complete the installation of the lock. The thought hit us all simultaneously. Norm had thrown them into the fire. I had read somewhere that a good bed of ashes should be left in a fireplace for a successful fire, but had overdone it to the point of not cleaning it for about two weeks. You can imagine the mess Cinderella had to sift through to find the missing screws. We assured Norm he never would find them, but he searched until he found them and by dinner time the lock was giving us black looks from both sides. Right then I decided a slide bolt would do for the other two doors, but since they were insulated it's almost impossible to open them anyway, so as yet the bolts are among the missing along with storm sash and other items too numerous to mention. I must lock that door sometime to see how it works. Hope the heat didn't melt the screws out of shape.

The Colonel Attacks The Attic

The company which manufactured the type of insulation bats Norm bought for the attic had very definite ideas how their product should be installed. In each bat was a slip of paper with pictures and captions which should have been a cinch for an old "Life" reader. Norm glanced at the slips then tossed them into the fireplace and said he was going to do the job in a more original fashion. He could insulate without pictures.

I was at the sink in my trusty red flannelled nighty cussing silently at the egg yolks which seemed to be delighting in sticking to the plates when Norm reached over with the stapling gun he had hired for the duration of "Operation Insulation" and tried out the gun. It worked and I let out a loud protest and he grinned and said, "Just testing Bun," and with that, he and his chemical shirt went charging up the narrow stairs with insulation clutched in both arms. He didn't get far. The load was too much for the narrow stairs so Norm backed down, eyes bright with a new more daring plan which included the dishwasher.

My instructions were to leave the dishes (that part sounded good) and run, not walk to the attic, open the window facing the barn and lean out. I ran as instructed, tore open the sash, and leaned out into the ten above zero weather and was thankful for the red flannel between me and it. Down below, Hopalong Cassidy Smith was busily fashioning a lasso of what I deemed to be part of my new clothesline. My job was to catch the lasso at great danger to life and limb, then lower one end to the ground. Then Hoppy would fasten his end of the rope onto the insulation and I was to pull it up through the attic window. For a solid hour I was up there pulling bats in through the window. Once Norm stepped on his end of the bat and gave me such a jerk I almost fell out on my head. I began to complain of overexposure and had I known it at

187

the time I might have stayed on and become "Miss Antifreeze of 1951." Why let Chicago take the honors. However, my engine was perking on coffee instead of gin so I might not have fared as well. When the complaints became louder and longer Norm had the audacity to ask if I was losing my sense of humor. Ever since Reader's Digest came out with an article a month or so ago stating that people with humor were normal, and in some cases even intelligent, I have taken a new lease on life. Wade read the article too and remarked that he hoped I wouldn't take it too seriously. Whenever Mom takes to the typewriter the whole place takes on a slightly "You Can't Take It with You Air" and his boyish heart cries out in protest. In Wade's youth I was far more apt to take to the vacuum cleaner, but after ten long, clean years, I found out they didn't pay off, so we'll try this for the next ten and see what happens.

At last, all the bats were upstairs and Norm shouted for me to wait up there for him. I did for the simple reason I couldn't have left if I wanted to. He came up the stairs, ignored the light switch in passing and asked where I was. My colorful costume was helpful in the search, and I was duly thanked and then allowed to seek the warmth (?) below.

Square Head

We had our lunch to the tune of the stapling gun. The boys kept running to the attic and then back reporting progress. Punchy came down once shaking his head and telling me he didn't think I was going to like it. That was no surprise to me. I was geared not to like the job from the moment Norm announced his intentions of insulating the attic. After lunch, I couldn't endure the suspense any longer, so I went upstairs to confirm Punchy's dim view of the job.

In other attics and I say this with longing in my heart, the insulation runs up and down between the rafters. Not so the Smith attic. Ours runs all around the attic from ceiling to floor and since the attic is tremendous, you have no idea how frightening it appears. It looks saggy, baggy and spooky. I thought maybe Edgar Allan Poe had been up there with Norm helping to create a horror chamber. Norm stood there, hands on hips, very much on the defensive and waited for me to express an opinion. I wanted to be kind. I knew I should be kind. After all, what other husband would spend his time around Christmas fixing up the attic? None I hoped, unless they were to follow the printed instruction type. I ventured softly, "Isn't it sort of baggy?" I had used the wrong adjective. "Baggy?" he boomed, "I'm not finished with it yet. What do you mean baggy?" The boys stood by with solemn brown eyes sensing a crisis. I had discussed with a friend of mine the importance of kids feeling secure and Punchy, the quiet one, had taken it all in. He came over to me, pulled my ear down to his level and whispered loudly not to do anything to ruin Keith's feeling of security. It struck me very funny and I assured Punchy that it would take more than fuss about the attic to shatter his brother. It would take something like not having three meals a day, or not being called Fathead by his Dad. Either would have a devastating effect on the little man who really believes "we are what

189

we eat," and quite possibly that his head is fat. Speaking of heads, Keith has a very interesting one. It is round, firm, and covered with hair which has the knack of standing straight up on end. Early in his youth, Norm used to call him "square head" jokingly. Keith started to kindergarten right after Christmas one year and announced that he was going to keep his hat on in school, We went into the usual long parental explanation of why he shouldn't leave his hat on and it was several minutes before we had sense enough to ask him why. Children usually have reasons for doing things, if their parents would allow them to. Norm, a more experienced parent than I, asked Keith why he was going to leave his hat on. Keith gave us the look kids reserve for their parents, when they think their parents are being especially stupid and replied very cheerfully, "I don't want the kids to see the corners on my head."

A Simple Trip To Providence!

I might have known the old Buick would take a time like that to do us wrong. I was to have met Mother in Providence for dinner and a concert, leaving Norma at home with the boys. However, we were waterless, joyless and mentally depressed in general and a trip to the city and the vision of Mother's bathtub looming on the horizon gave birth to a horrible thought. Norma and the boys would go to Providence with me and stay at Mother's while she and I pursued culture.

Naturally the boys chose to dilly dally on the way home from school which got us off to a late start. We had the deep well cooker full of turkey soup, two quarts of milk and a box of crackers, as we knew Mother wouldn't be prepared for an invasion of this type.

We had been having trouble with the overhead door in the shed. It is only distantly related to the type we installed in the red barn back home. This one is a solid mass of green lumber which lifts up all in one piece and spends its entire life contracting and expanding with the fickle New England weather. On the day I speak of, we sallied forth expecting a bad time with the door, but it came down so easily that Keith, an innocent bystander, got the full weight of it on his small nose. He howled with the injustice of it all, so we were off to a crying start.

As we raced down Route 44 the windows kept steaming up, so Punchy kept cleaning off my side with his mittens. I thought it was the turkey soup, as it was piping hot when we put it in the car, We smelled like the Cordon Blu on tour.

Pretty soon, a smoky odor assailed my nostrils. I said in great exasperation, "Norma, if you have to chain smoke, how about opening a window?" Her injured voice came ricocheting from the depths of the back seat, "Phil, I haven't had a cigarette since we left home." My brain began to function about that time, so I brought the car to a fast stop. As soon as we stopped, smoke began to pour in around us and Punchy had the presence of mind to suggest that we get out before the car exploded. He's a wonderful kid in an emergency (I'm all for more of them).

He was out of the car in a flash and had lifted the heavy hood and shouted, "Mrs. S. I hope your fire insurance is all paid up." That kid should know by now what a demon for insurance his father is, so I assured him everything was under control. Keith's only concern was the soup. We stood by the roadside waiting for the car to burst into flames, but it didn't.

Several nice looking cars drove by without even looking, then an old jalopy tore by, used what brakes it had to stop, then backed up to where we were parked. The man jumped out and asked us what happened. We told him our problem and I must admit I resorted to some of my old tactics I had to use during the war, when Norm was in Africa and I used to run out of gas. Looks like I might as well brush up on them anyway as I'll no doubt end up with an "A" sticker again.

Our new found friend was prepared for any emergency. He got out a tow rope, gave me last minute instructions how to follow him and we were off to the nearest gas station, ten miles away. Nothing could have pleased Keith anymore. He lives in a world of his own where trucks and tractors and old jalopys far outnumber people and he was taking everything in. I knew he would be towing cars over my hooked rugs for a month to come.

We steamed into the gas station and before leaving us to the mercy of the gas station attendant our friend asked in a whisper, "Are you financially embarrassed?" I replied, "Constantly, but my daughter has money." He offered to float a loan but, but I assured him we could get the old car out of hock the next day for by that time we knew it would have to spend the night in the garage. He left us with some misgivings, but we were pleased to be amid civilization. We decided to call a cab to transport us out to Mother's.

The cab driver didn't mind us too much, but when he saw the array of food that accompanied us, he took an instant dislike to his job. I realized he was tired and hungry and the odor of that good soup annoyed him no end. We descended upon Mother's quiet neighborhood looking for all the world like one of the New York Time's neediest cases. Mother, one of the originators of the word punctual, met us at the door, hat on head, geared for another Smith emergency. I pulled her out with one arm, pushed the kids in with the other and said, "Come on, I'll explain everything on the way down." Seems like I have been explaining the Smith antics for the past fourteen years to Mother. Mother was highly philosophic. "Well you got here in time anyway," and with that was off onto a discussion of the symphony and how much we were going to do together this winter. Mother has a mental picture of her daughter. There is a large portrait of me and the caption reads, "She switched to Culture."

Back to Woodstock

The next morning found us boarding busses in search of the car. We hadn't thought to inquire what street the gas station was on, so we ended up calling the cab company. A droll voice answered, and I told the man to locate the driver, if possible, and find out where he had picked us up. A lot of shouting followed and then the droll voice asked, "Were you them dames with the food," and I replied, "Yes." It was positively thrilling to be identified so easily. "You's was at the corner of such and such a street," so I thanked him and hung up. We got onto a second bus which took us to where the trusty car was waiting. Never had that faded red and chipped shellac jitney looked so good to me.

We headed for home and Punchy kept telling us to step on it as he had to be at school by twelve noon. The kids in his room were going to play at the Academy and he was in agony lest he be late. Keith was worrying about missing his lunch at school. We dropped Punchy off lunch less at the Academy and took Keith to his room and the welcoming of his teacher. She hastened out to find a tray for Keith, so we left young Henry the Eighth surrounded by food and the obvious interest of his fellow classmates. Whether the interest in him was aroused by his sense of showmanship or his capacity for food, we didn't wait to find out. If the school lunch program finds a deficit at the end of the year, we have a faint inkling of who might be responsible.

Returning The Stapler

The day before Norm left to go back to Pennsylvania Mr. Stormsash stopped by to pick up the check. He seemed to be in a cheerful mood and as he walked away, check in hand, he looked back and said humorously, "After all, you want that sash on before spring." We nodded in agreement and Norm told me he thought Stormsash was about to go into action at long last.

Where the vacation had gone to, we didn't know. I thought of it as hiding in the dark recesses of the attic beneath a blanket of insulation, but I didn't want to appear ungrateful, so said nothing. I drove Norm to Providence to get on a bus and his parting words were to get that storm sash on and return the stapling gun to the lumber company. Norm had put a ten dollar deposit down for the use of it and if I had played it smart, I would be ten dollars richer. Richer is hardly the word. Norm even opened the window of the bus, dousing the occupants with a dash of cold air to remind me once more about the stapler. On that score I needed no reminding. For ten dollars I would push it all the way to Putnam with my nose.

During the war years, we had a lot of practice in saying goodbye, so we are two veterans by now. Besides Norm had a trip to New York all planned for the mid-term recess and that would be early in February. We hadn't been to New York together for several years, so Norm was full of plans. Before the second batch of Smiths came along, we used to go down to New York at Easter time every year. We always went by way of Trenton and stopped in to see our relatives on the way. Between Trenton and New York, however, there was an obstacle that Norm could never circumnavigate. It is the Walker Gordon dairy farm, a fabulous place where you can watch the cows being milked while you partake of the ice cream made from this selfsame milk. To Norm, a great ice cream lover, that spot is the epitome of everything clean, healthy and satisfying. As for me, I like my ice cream further away from the source of supply, but when the cows got to where they would look at me and say, "Hello Phyllis" I told Norm it was time to stop. The only thing that stopped us was the war and we haven't been back since. Wonder if the girls have forgotten me by now?

A week later, the stapler was still on the kitchen counter and as I had had four letters reminding me to return it. I took the boys to Putnam for haircuts and to return the stapler. It was a bitter cold winter day, one in which dark creeps up on you about four-thirty. I was dressed in my usual country attire, slacks and an old grey coat, plus my Betmar jockey cap which was the height of style several seasons ago. It was intended to be worn by sweet young things, but since I am no longer young or sweet or a thing, it looks horrible. I find too, that when you live on top of a hurricane hill you put your hat way down close to your eyebrows to get safely from the house to the barn and by that time you have forgotten the angle and go blithely on your way. I deposited the boys at their respective barbers and walked back to the car to get the stapling gun. I should say here and now that a stapling gun looks more like a Tommy gun than a Tommy gun does. I reached into the car, picked up the lethal looking weapon and started down the street. A cop came on the run and I stood there innocently until I realized I was the object of all the yelling. These two ladies had seen me dive into the car and come out with a gun and start down the street at a determined pace and I guess they thought for a moment Ma Barker was in town. If the cop hadn't been there I would have pointed the stapler at them and tried to make the noise that kids make that sounds like a machine gun going off. I must get the kids to teach me how that sound is made.

I hid the gun inside my coat and descended upon the lumber company office. Do you *think* they gave me ten dollars? Oh no. Ten dollars credit went down on a pink slip and that was the end of that. I was really disappointed as I had already planned how the money was to be spent.

I wrote Norm my tale of woe about the return of the gun and fact that he had a ten dollar credit at the lumber company. He answered that it was perfectly all right with him, but then of course he hadn't counted on spending the money for anything specific. He also said it was just like having money in the bank, and I wrote back and asked him how he knew. He answered that he remembered from a long time back, before Phyllis.

Planning For A New York Weekend

The letters then changed tempo, instead of instructions about the stapler, I began to receive detailed instructions of how to get to New York from Providence, when to leave Providence to get to New York, then how to reach the hotel when I got there. There was a strong emphasis placed on the word walk. I could walk very easily to the hotel from the bus station. After all, I didn't want to break my record for never having been in a taxi in New York did I? Since I couldn't answer that last query honestly, I didn't answer it at all. I'll probably end up a cab driver in my reincarnation. They claim you usually do end up as something completely foreign to your first life on earth. Norm thinks he'll be a banker dispensing loans instead of making them.

Grandma Smith came to stay with Norma and the boys as Norma was to leave for Texas while I was in New York. Of course none of us anticipated the great railroad sickness.

Chapter 6

MISCELLANEOUS ARTICLES FROM THE 50's

(1956)

I had been wanting one for four, going on five years. Or maybe it was five, going on six. I don't really remember how many years I have been wanting one.

It all happened very suddenly one wet April day. Joe, the man we buy our produce from, had one ice-cream chair kicking around his office. I had been admiring it twice a week for many weeks before Joe became aware of my passion for ice-cream parlor chairs. On this wet day I speak of, Joe loudly proclaiming the virtues of a crate of broccoli when he noticed my inattention. "You like dat?" he asked pointing a stubby finger at the object of my affections. I nodded solemnly, "Putta inna da truck" he ordered one of his drones, then went back to the broccoli with a vengeance. I bought the broccoli then went out to the Jeep and caressed the lone ice cream parlor chair.

I will spare my readers the unkind remarks that greeted my return to the Ranch with the chair. There was much to the "never look a gift horse in the mouthing," much ado about nothing, in fact, much of everything, but admiration for my latest acquisition. Seeking the peace and comfort of the "Black Ash", I picked up my ice-cream parlor chair and went home to Norm. Now there is a man who had eaten his weight in ice cream many times over and you would think he would automatically recognize an ice-cream parlor chair, a very good ice-cream parlor chair. He wasn't cruel or unkind. He just said, "I don't care, but what is it?" He looked null and void when I told him it was an ice-cream parlor chair and it wasn't and it hadn't cost him a cent. The last remark raised his suspicions immediately. I might sell my soul for a mess of pottage, but never for a bunch of broccoli, and never for an ice-cream parlor chair.

Norm has been living with me so many years that he knew what my next move would be. He suggested that the one chair might get lonesome all by itself and that I had better get another to keep it company. I thought it an idea of great merit and worthy of further consideration.

Two days later, we stopped at Mr. Limoge's antique parlor. We asked timidy if the had any ice-cream parlor chairs. We were escorted into a large barn, up a flight of stairs, and there hanging above our heads were more ice-cream parlor chairs than I ever dreamed existed. I tried not to appear too excited or pleased, but being obviously both, was easy prey for the Limoges'. I told them I had one ice-cream parlor chair and wanted three more to go with it. They wouldn't have showed any more emotion if I had said I wanted thirty more to go with the one I had. Then up came the ghastly question of money. "Seven-fifty" was the price per chair. I as temporarily immobilized. I had planned to pay five dollars apiece, and not one cent more. I said as much, and Mrs. Limoge said to call the next day as she would talk it over with Mr. Limoge and see "what he could do." We were just about to leave when Norm spied something that pleased him no end. It was a round table to go with the ice-cream parlor chairs. He loved it, he wanted to buy it. The idea of having a complete set got the best of him. In fact, he said if I would buy the set he would supply the ice cream to go with it. I didn't want the table. I just wanted a big round umbrella table to go with the umbrella I had inherited from Mother's estate. Norm said I could drill a hole in the top of the ice-cream table for the umbrella. He was determined to have the table. "How much?" I asked, and Mrs. Limoge said "Twelve-fifty." Norm was wearing his "a bargain at twice the price look", so I didn't interfere.

The next day I went back to Limoge's. What Mr. Limoge had to say would not make good, clean copy. The price was still seven-fifty per as there would be a big demand all summer long from the "summer people." They had me right where they wanted me. I paid a deposit on the chairs and brought one home with me. To me ice-cream parlor chair was an ice-cream parlor chair was an ice-cream parlor chair. You would be surprised. Their twisting and turnings can be so different, to say nothing of their legs and backs. Which was the bastard? I couldn't tell, but I knew that I would have to match the one Joe gave me or trade it in for one to match the three I bought. The next day I went back to Limoge's. I took the chair Joe had given me inside and told Mrs. Limoge my tale of woe. I asked if she would consider letting me trade in that one for a chair to match the three I had bought. She wouldn't say yes, and she wouldn't say no. She said she would have to ask her husband. I was so fascinated with finding a woman who had to ask her husband questions that I became so fouled up I bought a copper boiler to use for a trash can in our Connecticut kitchen. She asked me what I was going to use it for and I replied very honestly that it would be a good trash can for the Smith kitchen. "Nice kitchen," she said wickedly and I began to feel ill at ease and ashamed of being the kind of family that could fill a small boiler full of trash every day. Somehow the Jukes and Kale kaks didn't seem so remote anymore. I was allowed to leave my chair there and take another home with me and was to call next day to see what the Lord and Master had to say.

The next day WE went in to Limoge's. Mr. Limoge does not have horns, and does not breathe fire. He has cash register eyes, but aside from that is a big, silent man. He had made the decision to let me trade in my chair for one of his, but was annoyed to see me bringing back the two I had already bought. I was thankful that Norm was as big as Mr. Limoge. We all went upstairs in the barn and picked out four identical chairs. Even the table turnings matched the four chairs we picked out. Limoge was relieved, I was happy and Norm was broke. That night I went to sleep secure in the knowledge that I owned a real old fashioned ice-cream parlor set.

The next day, I didn't go to see Mr. Limoge. I didn't call Limoge and I didn't think about Limoge. I just admired the ice-cream parlor set.

Yesterday, Norm said to me, "Say Bun, why don't you go see that Turk in Anthony's." Not being interested in Turks anywhere, I asked him why. "That used to be an old ice-cream parlor," he said. I waited patiently. "He must have some old equipment around," Norm went on. I nodded in my own vague manner. "Why not have two ice-cream parlor sets?" Norm asked and I replied, "Why not."

Tomorrow I am going in to see that "Turk in Anthony's."

In this article written in 1957, Phyllis reflects on her pursuit of getting her book "It Was Nothing" finished and published. Now over 50 years later, her dream comes true.

"WILL I EVER FINISH MY BOOK"

I don't know why even now, that we had to be the first in our snug little society to feel the economic trend that was about to rock the nation. We began to recede with the recession just before Christmas and what worse time is there than just before Christmas?

We had hired a painter for a few days and he was well into his third week of employment when my husband called my attention to the fact that our income had not taken wings, but was literally grounded from then on. For one used to a very static income, small but steady, I was not about to fire the painter or change our standard of living overnight. In other words, I just couldn't take the recession seriously and I wasn't helped by the fact that all my playmates were going on their merry way with no great concern about the future. Keith, our thirteen year old son was far more concerned about the recession than I. He doesn't still believe in Santa Claus, but he knows somebody puts those packages under the tree, and that somebody was the same somebody who was trying to impress his Mother with the fact that things were bad on the financial home front. It must have been Keith who asked me why I didn't write my book and get it published so we eat during the holidays. I have been writing a book for twenty years, off and on, but now the chips were down and he felt I should get on the ball, write my book, get it published, so we could pay the painter and perhaps even burn the mortgage.

A few days before the holidays began, our fifteen year old son, Punch, called on the phone from school. Nobody has even accused either of the Smith brothers of being fleet of foot, but that is only because they have never seen Keith in action when the phone rings.

Whenever the phone rings, Bannister takes the back seat. The procedure goes like this. The phone rings and Keith lets out a real T.V. yell and says, "I've got it," and believe me he has. Unlike his mother, who suffers with a very severe case of telephobia, Keith loves to talk on the phone and is willing to divulge the most intimate details as to my whereabouts. I am either washing my hair, taking a bath, or, you guessed it. However, on this particular occasion I was not washing my hair, taking a bath, or, you guessed it. I was out looking for Sputnik, and if I ever find the disc jockey who told his listeners that Sputnik could be seen around six, I'll break a long playing record over his head. Anyway, Keith answered the phone and was charmed to inform his brother of my whereabouts. Eventually, Punch wanted to know if he could have a word with me (which always costs me money) and Keith said he didn't know if I could take time off to talk since I was writing a book. Punch asked, "What again?" Keith went on to say there were only twelve shopping days left until Christmas and we were broke. Punch said it was too bad we didn't live in New York so we could be one of the hundred neediest cases and Keith replied hopefully that there was always the Salvation Army. When I finally got on the phone Punch said, "Hello Grace, you don't have to get me that Jaguar for Christmas," and I said, "That isn't funny Punch," and he said, "Neither was the book, but it sold." He asked me what I was writing about and I said, "Just the usual your Dad, Keith, the dogs," and he said, "Good, we won't sue. Incidentally, is there any sex in your book?" I said, "Just male and female, and Punch groaned and said, "It will never sell," and on that happy note, we said goodbye, then Keith got back on the phone to find out just when Punch got out of school and Punch said he would be home for his Christmas vacation starting on the sixteenth and Keith said, "You mean your no Christmas vacation," and Punch agreed.

What makes people write books anyway? A great many high minded people write books because they feel they have a message to bring the world. Others write to try and reform the world at large. Some write because of ego frustration, but the real lowbrows like myself, have but one purpose in mind and that is, money. We all have our secret desires and ambitions. One of our best friends yearns to walk thru a room full of Gina Lollabrigida's in his bare feet, and he isn't even considered queer. All I want to do is walk thru a room full of one dollar bills in my bare feet. If Menninger sees this, we both will have had it, but as of now, we are both in our bare rooms carrying on life in as normal a manner as we know how.

I was well started on my book when I suddenly realized it had no plot, no continuity, and no sales appeal. I thought to remedy this serious situation by the simple medium of sending out my unrelated chapters as separate little units. Surely, the slicks were dying for this kind of fluff to take the edge off the recession, and perhaps even cause a little laughter in this, our darkest hour. I couldn't have been more wrong, and being wrong is something I have devoted most of my life to. Now I am back to the book and it is a nice feeling. One rejection slip is much easier to take than twelve, and look at the postage I will save.

One trouble with books is that they have to have titles. I don't know who started this practice, but have you ever seen a book which just says "Book" on the jacket. No half naked woman either, just a plain cover reading, "Book." It might be a whole raw approach to the world of books. I have even owned books on "What to name the baby" but have you ever seen a book on "What to name the Book?" I haven't and with this in mind, we ran a little contest right here on the home front. The boys were full of ideas, and they were all pretty bad. Punch's last one intrigued me. It was "Too Little, Too Late" but was rejected because it was too obvious. Keith came up with "Pomfret Place" but since we didn't live in Pomfret we had to reject that one. It finally evolved itself into "It Was Nothing" and believe me, it isn't.

I never think of myself as a joiner, except when it comes to Book Clubs, and I am the joiniest joiner possible. I attribute this to the fact that we have always lived in the country and running to a library is not always too convenient. Another thing is I become attached to the books I read and someday, when I am an old lady, I fully intend to reread every book in my own library. I don't spend money in the beauty parlor, which is very obvious to everyone who knows me, so books and book clubs are my vice. I even buy books in book stores and department stores, in short I buy books, read books and keep books. This mania for collecting books is good for the community too as we are consistently employing carpenters to build shelves, painters to paint them, and women to dust them. When we run out of shelves, we build onto the house, it's that simple…. simple, but expensive.

As a book owner, you naturally become the ready prey of book borrowers, and some of the nicest people borrow books, and if the string you tie to the book is long enough, you often get your book back.

In thinking back on my childhood, I realize that my Mother was way ahead of her years in that I had a most lenient and permissive atmosphere in which to grow up. My Mother put up with my mood swings, my day dreaming, my friends, and the only thing I do remember being reprimanded about was my natural talent for overdoing things. In these days, I would probably have been hauled off to some clinic and taught to under do things, but since such help was not deemed necessary in those days, I continued with my overdoing. This trait of character was really pretty obvious at the time I was married. Not only did I get a man, but three children to boot. Now in my defense, I want to say that I was not looking for a man, much less a man with a family, but we met one summer and he decided that I was just what is needed. I was young, strong, and very pliable. He needed a wife and the kids needed a mother and he could bring me up along with the kids. He didn't propose, he just informed me that we would get married the following summer. I do clearly remember one edict she issued. If this was my choice for my future, I would have to stick to it, make a go of it, and that there would be no running home to Mother. I did stick to it and made a go of it for about five years before I ran home to Mother. It was terribly disconcerting to have my husband help me pack the car. It wasn't like it was in the movies at all. He and the three kids waved a happy goodby and before I had gone ten miles, I was wondering what the hell I was going home for anyway, but pride kept me on the highway. My Mother was really startled to se me at her back door and I am sure that Typhoid Mary would have received more of a welcome. I got no sympathy whatsoever, in fact, I was lucky to get my dinner. I was granted the use of the guest room for one night with the understanding that I would leave first thing in the morning for home and my responsibility. The only free advice I had was that I should have a baby of my own. Nothing could have been further from my mind at the time. I drove home, found Norm and the kids happily eating their dinner and nobody seemed surprised to see me. Norm inquired about my Mother, etc., and I told him she was fine and I had the poor taste to tell him what she had recommended. He seemed very pleased at the prospect and remarked that I had come to the right place and I got a little annoyed at him for leering at me in anticipation.

Life went on very smoothly after that for about a month. I awoke one morning to the horrible realization that I was not going to have a baby of my own. I couldn't believe it. I had made up my mind, the cooperation had been one hundred percent and I wasn't pregnant. All day long I seethed with emotion or frustration or whatever you seethe with when you think you should be pregnant and you're not. I could hardly contain myself until we had dinner and the kids were in bed. I aroused Norm from under the evening paper and broke the news as gently as I could to him that he would have to see a doctor. He wanted to know why and I replied, "Because I'm not pregnant that's why." Now if I had been older and more experienced, I never would have chosen an approach like that. Nothing in the world makes a man madder than to have his virility questioned and especially a man who has three kids already asleep upstairs. He leaped out of his chair and said, "For C .... sake, what are you talking about?" but I was overdoing it as usual and asked if it was because he was too old or what. The poor guy must have been all of thirty-seven at the time and this last suggestion was almost too much for him. He got so angry and suggested that I see a doctor, but then he cooled off and said he was sorry and that he was sure I could and would produce a child in the very near future. As always, he was right. I ordered a girl and got a boy, which was par for the course.

My Mother was right about the baby. Nothing welds a family together like a baby, and two babies make escape an utter impossibility. First we were five and now we were seven. I began to wonder if it was going to be seven come eleven. As I look back on it, we were quite a formidable aggregation. I can't remember that either of us converging on their respective doorsteps. One Christmas we decided to be smart and stay home and it was the best Christmas we ever had. The tree caught on fire, Keith fell all the way downstairs on his new tractor, doing all kinds of damage to the new paint job, and our dog disappeared. It was a red letter holiday all right. I think it was during that vacation that Bob,

Norm's oldest son, made a very wise observation. I made some remark about the family and Bob said, "This is no family, it's just a bunch of individuals," and he was right.

If I had my life to live over again, I wouldn't, but since I have no choice in the matter, I can't say it hasn't been fun. Just imagine three kids to practice on before you had any of your own. Nothing my boys do can surprise me, and they have learned to accept this fact. When other Mothers are eating their hearts out, I am relaxed and calling the next play. The fact that my two boys are almost exact replicas of their older brothers helps no end, too. How this came about will always baffle me, but what chance did my poor little genes have anyway. Sometimes I wonder if I really gave birth to these monsters.

Human nature being what it is, the two older boys are married and have little monsters of their own, so before my own two leave and biology catches up with them, I find myself overrun with grandchildren. I tell you there is no escape. I was complaining about my future one day and how life had been just one pair of mittens after another and Keith said, "It couldn't have happened to a nicer person," and that softsoap kept me going for another twenty-four hours.

Sometimes I get so tired of living in this athletic paradise I want to throw in the sponge. We live in New England which is very famous for having four definite seasons every year, but even if we lived in Tibet I could tell when the seasons change. Now my system is all based on balls, and has nothing to do with time, tide, or outer space. Before the first leaf changes in the fall, a football appears and the Smith brothers are clobbering each other in two-man football. The Giants take over the household and then suddenly the football becomes a basketball and winter is upon us. Just when you get to know all the Celtics by name, the baseball gloves appear and every morning when you pick up the house, you pick up gloves of various sizes, and shapes. Spring has sprung and another baseball season is upon us. I really don't need a calendar at all. Life is just one big athletic contest, and I seem to be the only consistent loser. You would think that after twenty years I would have adjusted to this state of affairs. Forewarned is forewarned and what other bride do you know of that got a box-seat in Fenway Park for a wedding present from her husband? It was the nicest thing he could think of to do for me, and I still maintain I am the only woman alive who spent her honeymoon in Fenway Park. Still think I am suffering from being knocked out by a fly ball which landed on my head during a game. Norm was so interested in the game that an usher had to call his attention to the fact that I was sprawled out cold in my wedding present seat. Once I had revived, I was taken to task for interrupting a very unique play being staged in the outfield.

One very fortunate thing about my marriage was that I was not looking for romance, so when romance didn't appear I wasn't hurt, upset or even baffled. One night when we were out on our way to a pro basketball game, I saw a really gorgeous harvest moon and called Norm's attention to it. He eyed the full moon carefully and said wistfully, "It looks just like a basketball." See what I mean? When my boys were little their playpen was short on playschool toys, but long on balls. The older boys spent a great deal of time bouncing a volleyball off Keith's head and now they wonder why he isn't distinguishing himself in his studies.

This winter something new has been added and that something new is Bonnie Pruden. It seems to me that every morning now is Thursday. I know it really isn't, it just seems that way. Bonnie has convinced Norm that we are, in fact, a mess. I know it, but I am willing to accept the fact. However, now when the T.V. gets switched on at seven, we groan and know that when Bonnie appears, we appear or else. Punchy is lucky. He is away at school. It doesn't help any to have three dogs walking over you and drooling on you when you are trying to get your blood circulating in the right direction. What blood? I gave some serious thought to trying to redeem some I had left at the last drawing. I can't see that any of us has improved with the exercising, but I feel that it can't do any harm.

Today I am home alone and decided it would be a good time to write. Norm and the boys have left for a place called "Jug End Barn" and judging from the brochure, they will love it. One thousand four hundred acres devoted to sports, every kind of sport known to man, and always the possibility of dreaming up a new one. One of my friends told me it was a place where women go to meet men. I repeat, every sport known to man. I did feel that I should warn my six foot sons about all the Marjorie Morningstar's who might be lurking about. I told Keith that if any dame proposed to him, he should tell her that he had to wait until he got out of grammar school. I figured Punch was old enough to fight for his own life, but I wondered how hard he would fight if the opportunity presented itself. Norm, I wasn't worried about. I just hoped that Bonnie Pruden would be there for his sake. They have been gone for three hours now. I have picked up six baseball gloves, done the dishes, made the beds, done the laundry, breathed deeply twelve times and am about to collapse.

I might not be suffering with any of the ailments I hear about all the time on radio and T.V. I haven't got hyper-tension, hyper acidity, tired blood or super anahist, and since I can brush three times a day, I can even pick out my own brand of tooth paste, and if I want to paste my teeth or powder them, I'm going to. However, my freedom ends here because we have three dogs. Don't ask me why, except we always did like seven as a number. When our three older kids left home, we got three dogs, and I am not insinuating in any way that dogs can replace children. There are things to be said about both however, good and bad. Dogs don't bring home bad report cards, but on the other hand, kids don't shed, so one offsets the other. Having boys and dogs at the same time does become a bit of an endurance contest at times, especially when the dogs you own don't think of themselves as dogs. I have known for two years that Riley sleeps in Keith's bed, and I have become adjusted to the fact that dogs usually sleep in boy's beds. The thing I am having difficulty adjusting to is having a dog in my bed.

It all started last summer when a friend of mine asked me to take care of a dachshund pup for about ten days. I agreed as one dog more or less wouldn't make too much difference. However, Norm was not as carried away with the little girl as I was, and was glad it was only for ten days.

PUSH BUTTON PARADISE

One very definite impression I picked up while traveling in Europe last fall is the rather low esteem in which the average American woman is regarded by her sex overseas. The very fact that we flock to Europe alone, in groups, with or without our husbands, and take pictures of anything and everything in sight hasn't added to our popularity either. Years ago, it was easy to blame Hollywood for our being misunderstood abroad, but now that they have seen so many of us, I feel that I must come to our defense. Here, in a nutshell, is a rough draft of what we are thought to be like, for the most part. We start the day off with a waking up pill to counteract the affect of the sleeping pill we took the night before. From our beds we push a series of buttons, the first of which ejects the poor husband so he can catch the commuter train. During the morning, we drive around in our cars, meet our playmates for lunch at some smart club, pick up the kids up at school, and then go home. After the kids have romped around for an hour or so, there is another pill to calm your shattered nerves. Shortly thereafter, it is time to shower, jump into the basic black dress, mix the cocktails, and be reclining on the divan when the commuter arrives home. He of course, is in a playful mood after having drinks on the train with the boys, so after smoking a few of those twenty-thousand filter tip cigarettes, you kiss the kids goodby and take off for a round of evening parties. The next day, the cycle begins all over again, or so they seem to think.

It's true, up to a certain point, that we do live in a push button paradise, but one has to be on hand to push the buttons and to let the constant stream of repair men in and out of paradise, so the end result is … paradise lost.

When not washing or ironing or cooking or dusting or sewing or papering or painting or polishing the silver or chauffeuring the kids around, there are numerous little jobs to keep the housewife out of mischief. One of those falls under the simple term of gardening. Translated it means, reading all the seed catalogs, ordering the seeds, spading the garden, planting the, weeding the garden, watering the garden, fertilizing the garden, harvesting the garden, and now in this age of enlightenment, freezing the produce of the garden. That's just one tiny sample of a seasonal extra. We live in what might be called a "charming" old house in the country. This is an adjective used primarily by those living in neat, compact little ranch houses, which could be heated adequately with the heat which escapes from the old "charmer" daily. Well anyway, the old house is so charming that on a quiet night you can hear the moths hatching in the cracks between those marvelous old, wide floorboards. Just the business of moth detecting, chasing and spraying can keep a gal on the go. Every so often, when life gets really dull, we engage in a little practice known as "cleaning under the rugs." It sounds very basic when you say it, but before the process is over we are always embroiled in a real domestic crisis. This is a job that cannot be done alone, and since the cleaning woman was scratched way back in '52, the poor husband becomes a party to the venture. The ideal set-up is for both the husband and wife to be armed a vacuum cleaner. We were a two vacuum family long before we became a two Ford family for the simple reason that we have always had more dirt than money. First of all, the furniture has to be moved off the rug and out of the way. This usually involves a little chipped paint which can always manage to irritate the wife. The rug is then folded back a foot or two and you go to work on those charming old cracks. Meanwhile, the man of your dreams is proceeding full speed ahead and seems to be taking up most of the Ozite carpet pad into the bag of his high pressure cleaner. This proves so irritating that the wife shuts off her cleaner and when she hears a terrible noise coming from "his cleaner". She shouts for him to shut the darn thing off. The T.V. blaring away upstairs doesn't help matters any, but you finally establish contact and he shuts his cleaner off. You are big enough to allow him the pleasure of deliberate calculation and the astounding deduction that the bag should be emptied. This just isn't the time for "I could have told you that," but you think it over secretly and relish the knowledge, but manage to recover in time to suggest that he empty your bag too. You then sneak out to the kitchen for a quick cup of coffee. The bag emptying is done in jig-time and once again you are both back at the controls. His cleaner sounds terrible. You hate to keep harping on it, but when you can see smoke billowing out of his cleaner, you once again establish contact and get him to turn off the switch. By now his pride is shattered and he can't understand why his cleaner is behaving so badly. Once again, he goes outside, opens the bag, turns on the switch, and low and behold out blows the rest of the rug pad. Then he decides his cleaner is just too powerful and that he shouldn't work on the pad anymore, especially since the New York Giants are due to dash across the T.V. screen almost any minute. You tell him not to feel too badly, what he didn't pick up in his cleaner the moths would probably get anyway. He leaves for the poor man's Yankee Stadium leaving you to swab down the deck. We always try to drown the little scamps we don't pick up in the cleaner. After the deck dries, the spraying program takes over that is if you can find the spray and the spray can the same weekend. This demands great synchronization and planning, but a few times we have been lucky. Once the spray is dry you feel a compelling urge to get the room back in order, but years of practice have told you the furniture can't be moved until the goal posts come down, so you collapse with the Sunday Times to outwait the Giants.

Before flexing your muscles, a la Bonnie Pruden, to be ready for hoisting furniture, the rug must be placed back on the remainder of the pad, so that no side of the pad shows. Can I help it if every rug pad we have ever owned always stretches out somehow and makes covering it on all four sides a human impossibility? Several times a year we trim off the edges, but every time the pad shows on some other side. I know this sounds mathematically impossible, but nevertheless it happens.

It is now six o'clock, so you straighten out your basic Mother Hubbard and head for the kitchen. All you have to do now is, set the table, prepare the dinner, serve the dinner, clear the table, do the dishes, help the kids with their homework, argue with the kids about taking baths, feed three dogs, watch, watch Steve Allen, and so to bed. Remind me to buy some of those pills will you?

Phyllis M. Smith
Sunnybank
East Woodstock, Connecticut

213

"WHERE HAVE YOU BEEN"

Not too long ago, a famous lady writer suggested that all married people omit the word "always" from their conversation, thus insuring a long and happy married life. In this utopia of happily married people, the husband would no longer say to his wife, "You always leave the cap off the toothpaste." The wife should never say to her husband, "Why do we always have to go to see your Mother?" By the frequent use of that word, marriages totter and fail, caps are never put back on toothpaste and mother-in-laws become old ogres. Eliminate that word and your marriage will be as secure as if it was stashed away in the safe deposit at the bank.

I want to go that lady writer one better and suggest the elimination of four words which to my mind are far more infuriating and potent than "always." I am all for getting rid of that trite old question, "Where have you been?"

As a bride, I asked that question once, but never again. My husband taught at a large prep school nine miles from our home. One night he came home a little later than usual, and I asked where he had been and he answered, "Nowhere." Then I asked him who he had seen and he replied, "No one." To my knowledge, he is the only man in captivity that could drive eighteen miles and not go anywhere and mingle with several hundred students and teachers and still not see anybody. It was such a unique thing that I pursued it no further and every time I hear some wife asking, "Where have you been?" I wish her husband would give her a similar reply and wise her up. Nothing can be more shattering to a man who has been beating his brains out all day, long enough to keep the family clothed and fed than to be greeted at the door with, "Where have you been?"

Now if every husband had a stock reply, he would save himself a lot of grief. Once he tried explaining honestly, he could get himself terribly involved. I am thinking now of one friend who has the "Where have you been?" habit. They have been married six years and they have six children. The next time she asks, her husband answer, "Down at the fertility clinic," or something equally improbable. It would be a long time before his wife asked him that question again.

Let us now consider the man who usually drops off at the local pub before going home to the little woman. When she gives out with the third degree questioning, he could say, "I've been to the W.C.T.U. meeting. That should shut the little woman up or at least give her food for thought.

Then we have the commuter, a hale and hearty soul who boards the Long Island Railroad twice a day. As usual, there is a wreck. He isn't killed, but is a little late in getting home. The shrew he hasn't tamed in ten years of commuting meets him at the door with, "Where have you been?" He should say, "I walked home," and let her hear about the wreck over the radio. It would be much easier on his ulcers.

Another type hard to cope with is the suspicious wife who thinks her spouse mentally and constitutionally incapable of coming right home after work. For him there is no hope. They could move to a desert island or else she could clean up the proverbial question and ask, "Where have you been?"

Next comes a wife who is married to a big wheel in the publishing business. There is no telling where this character has been, and all in the line of duty. When his wife asks, "W.H.Y.B.?" he could answer, "Not out with Kathleen Windsor, "which immediately unties the hard knot which is tied in her stomach, but quickly reties itself when she wonders which of the other good looking ones he might have been out with. How do men in that field get wives in the first place, not to mention the second, third or fourth?

We spent one winter in the Green Mountains on a ranch where we were snowbound most of the winter. Nobody was late for lunch at noon if they could possibly avoid it, as it was buffet style and was strictly survival of the fittest. A friend's husband got stuck in the snow and was five minutes late for lunch on the memorable day I speak of. She asked in a loud voice, "Where have you been?" Nobody cared really, but for lack of anything better to do, waited for his answer. "Down to Arthur Murray's," he replied and did a quick samba over to the denuded buffet table. She hasn't asked him any foolish questions lately.

By now I hope I have proved just how infuriating this question can be when asked of the man of the house, the breadwinner, the father of your children, that joyless creature who leaves home before eight in the morning and comes home at night only to be asked, "Where have you been?" Forget those four words girls and you'll be happier than Boggie and Becall, Dagwood and Blondie, and all your married friends put together.

Here it is five after six and the station wagon has just pulled into the driveway. I wonder where he has been. I can wonder, can't I?

During 1950 – 1954 the Smith family lived in Vermont as Norm worked at Spring Lake Ranch. The Ranch was a "halfway house" for emotionally challenged people. A magazine named "The Splash" was published bi-monthly.

HOME FOR THE HOLIDAYS

(1951)

Over the river and through the woods to Smith's house we went. It would have been better if we had gone to Grandmother's house. I speak of that festive and time-honored holiday known as Thanksgiving.

We left the Ranch in typical Smith fashion with an assortment of kids, luggage, cartons and paper bags. Norm suggested that we take Mittens home with us, so at the moment of departure, we had to scurry around and find that ball of fluff that was parked beneath the porch of the Black Ash. Keith lured her out and we were off for Connecticut.

To prevent boredom and guerilla warfare from breaking out in the back seat, Norm decided some tutoring was in order. So far, the magic formula for teaching Keith things easily hasn't been discovered, so you can imagine him learning things in the old Buick. We had a few close calls when Keith announced mildly during Arithmetic class that five and five made fifteen. Things like that can really upset the General and are very bad for his ulcers. After math class, Punchy held forth with some geography. Norm and I concluded that either our world had changed completely or else we were a couple of dumb heads. Punchy gave up in disgust and went back to his Atlas and let us wallow in our own ignorance. By then, Keith was sound asleep no doubt from the exertion of making fifteen out of five and five.

We thought we might get by the Howard Johnson's near Brattleboro, but both boys are equipped with radar which sends their gastric juices into a flood whenever we are within a five mile radius of one such restaurant. We charged in and made light work of numerous grilled frankfurters, ice cream sodas and popcorn balls.

The next stop was in Southbridge where I have been shopping for food since moving to Connecticut. Each boy latched onto a cart and in no time at all, they duplicated, and some instances, tripled everything I needed to buy for the few days we would be home. You can well imagine the scene of separating and returning to the shelves the surplus food. It did nothing to improve our popularity with the manager and checker. What was left added up to fifteen dollars and being penniless as usual, I sent Punchy out to the car to get some money from the General. In one mad moment of recklessness and devil may-care indifference, he parted with a five dollar bill, and sent Punchy in with it. As the crow flies, it wasn't more than a fifth of a mile to where the ar was parked, but I wasn't a crow planning on flying, but I did some cawing. Fortunately, Punchy is the type who keeps a closed zipper on his wallet, and he was only too glad to loan me the rest at three percent interest. Norm eyed the big bags and allowed as how that amount of food couldn't possibly have cost fifteen dollars. I was too weary to go into the matter of inflation, but when we go home at Christmas he will do the shopping and see for himself what goes on behind his back in a grocery store.

The Smith house sits high on a hill, a typical leaky old farmhouse designed to delight the eye and make the oil man a rich man in one cold winter. There is a cold, austere look about it that we haven't been around long enough to do away with. So far, we have no great feeling for the place and feel like strangers within its portals. However, we own it and it is bulging with Smith with Smith possessions, so it is home, if in name only. Upon entering the back door, you are greeted with the longest, coldest array of white porcelain seen this side of an appliance store. Theoretically, I am an emancipated woman, but then I have Norm to contend with. Nothing works when Norm is around except Nor,. It was with this in mind that he left me in the salesroom and wended his way down cellar to start the oil burner. It was a miraculous thing indeed when the burner started up without protest, and if I hadn't discovered a draft about the feet, this story might never have been written.

The Smith brothers always dash for their playroom and set up the electric train. In short order, they have it clanging around the tracks and belching smoke and whistling loudly and gaily. I get the washer and dryer tuned up, and the Smiths are at home.

The above mentioned draft hit my ankles as I walked into the living room, and upon looking down the cellar stairs, I saw that the cellar windows were open. I told Norm and he leaped for the nearest hammer and said, "No sooner said than done," and started at a furious pace to close the cellar windows. I went back to my friends in white, happy in the knowledge that the Super Chief was in full action upstairs and Norm was in the cellar for a while.

Many times since, I have tried to reconstruct the events leading up to the big catastrophe. Punchy flew into the kitchen with haggard eyes and said, "Daddy wants you down the cellar." I raced down and found our hero with one large thumb stuck into the bottom of the oil tank. He was covered with oil and smelled like the Atlantic Refining Company. The cellar looked dirty, oily and worse for wear. The General looked the same. His green eyes pleaded with me to do something clever, and in a hurry. He was half stooped over me in a puddle of oil and had been that way for half an hour. He gasped, "Bring me a cork or something so I can get my thumb out of here." I made tracks for the nearest whiskey bottle which was poised dejectedly in the trash barrel. It pretended it was going to stay, and the minute Norm straightened up, the cork let loose, and he was recoated. He quickly put in his thumb again and hollered at me, as though I was the hired help, to do something. I am never good in emergencies, but I knew better than to laugh. I found a clothespin and offered that to Norm. I should have left right then because I soon found myself holding the oil back while the General made a square pin fit a round hole. It worked, and we crawled upstairs exhausted. I thought Norm was going to bop Keith when he came meandering downstairs, looked at his father, then at me and asked, "What happened to him?"

It all happened during operation window. All went well until he wedged himself into the corner with the oil storage tank. That corner was never designed to accommodate two tanks. His foot slipped and he stepped onto the little copper pipe which leads from the tank to the burner. Then it was all over but the shouting.

The plumber came that night and cast a jaundiced eye about the cellar. He announced that he wouldn't touch the repair job until we had the tank siphoned out. The oil man thought it would be easier to siphon out the plumber. We were at a complete impasse until our good friend and neighbor, came over to pass the time of day and spent the night with us. He is a mill maintenance man and a wizard at repair jobs. He suggested a little gadget called an "Easy Out" to remove the end of the broken pipe. He took the remaining pipe and rethreaded it, and in a few hours, all was well again.

The next morning the phone rang and I said to Norm, "You answer it. Word has probably gotten around that you found oil on your property." I won't tell you what he said.

IT WAS NOTHING

(1957)

It was nothing. The year 1957, that is. We built a new addition on our house, I got a part-time job, went to Europe, Babo turned green, and they still haven't found out where the yellow went. I still it was nothing. Since this is almost 1958 and there are only seventeen shopping days until Christmas, to say nothing of paying off a loan at the bank, I had better get started on this pot boiler. I won't go back to January as that was a very dull month. I made a stab at having a "Do It Yourself" nervous breakdown, but the attempt was highly unsuccessful, since even a common cold in this family is regarded as very unsportsmanlike. Did you ever try to fall apart in a family of future Olympic athletes.

I'll never forget Friday February 1st as long as I live. It was one of those wet foggy days when even the socially adjusted feel slightly manic. I had spent the day writing checks to "The Book of the Month, The Flower of the Month, The Record of the Month, The Fruit of the Month and The End of the Month" clubs, and was in a state of near collapse, both literally and figuratively. I hid the checkbook in a new place and decided it was time for a drink even if it wasn't five o'clock. I was happily swilling down my second drink when my friend Slats called. Every Friday night Slats calls and I can usually tell by the greeting what kind of weekend it is going to be. For the past two months the greeting has gone something like this, "Now Mother Smith, get the skis waxed and we'll get in some skiing tomorrow afternoon." This is of course music to my ears. I haven's been on skis since I split my heat at Split Rock about fourteen years ago. However, at the beginning of the New Year, Slats had decided that a "Back to Health" move was in order and we have been pursuing health madly every weekend since. So far, we haven't overtaken it, but while there is life, there is Slats, so we might make it yet.

On this particular Friday the greeting was, "Hello, Smith," and I knew instinctively something was in the wind. Slats went on to say she was about to receive some back pay from a jewelry firm she used to work for and that this money was to be used for a trip to Europe. I was overcome and said, "Slats, that's wonderful, but you can't go without me, and I haven't got any money." I then remarked jokingly that I should get a job and earn some money, Slats replied, "I'll give you a job, Smith; I need part-time help in the office and it might as well be you as any other jerk." I overlooked the inference and asked, "How will we get there?" "Fly," retorted Slats, and I promised to get a new broom. Before hanging up, Slats said, "There's just one thing, Smith, don't get pregnant and spoil our trip," and I answered, "Remember your religion, Slats."

I first met Slats about three years ago. We liked each other from the start. She represented everything I had missed in life and I represented to her what she hadn't missed. Slats pulled a real switch inasmuch as she had worked in New York, had her fling, then came home to live and be a country girl again while gainfully employed in any big city within a fifty mile radius. We became good pals and it was fortunate for me that she liked children, since we always manage to have a couple hanging around our house. All one winter, she helped me chauffeur kids to all kinds of athletic contests, dances, parties, but all the while it was understood that some day, if I wasn't too decrepit, I would do the same for her.

Right now I should tell you that Slats is ten years younger than I. It sounds a lot better than saying I am 10 years older than Slats. One Saturday while attending some function at the school my son Keith darkens five days a week, we all became aware of the fact that the older boys were eyeing Slats with very appreciative eyes. Keith was marveling aloud at our being friends, especially since Slats was younger than I. I explained that I wasn't ready for the junkyard yet and that it was possible to have friends in different age groups. Keith gave the matter as much thought as he was capable of at the time, then turned to us with somber brown eyes and said, "I'll tell you, Mom, Slats has got "It" physically, but you've got it mentally." We were both so amused and flattered that it didn't occur to Slats to wonder what was wrong with her mind or for me to wonder what was wrong with my physique. I found out a long time ago that you can't have everything.

On Sunday it occurred to me that my husband might just wonder where I was all day Monday, so I bearded the lion in his den. As usual, the lion was fast asleep under the Sport section of the New York Times, and once aroused couldn't have been less interested in the world shattering news that the old girl was going to become a career girl. He allowed as how I could go to Europe with Slats if I earned the money and said that he would match anything I could earn. He fully expected the job to last about two weeks, but never let on last October that he regretted making the offer of double or nothing. We were right in the midst of a large expansion program known at first as "The New Addition" but months later, as "Smith's Folly". All available funds, ours and the bank's, were being devoured by the new wing, but "Addition" or "Folly" I was Europe bound and the family accepted the fact.

Several years ago, in a patriotic moment, I had purchased a $1000 war bond and it had been stashed away to ripen and then to take Punch (our 15-year old son) to Europe. I had planned on the bond and the boy maturing about the same time and I wanted so much for him to see Europe through rose-colored glasses instead of rose-colored eyeballs. Last summer was the time I picked, but when I suggested a student tour to Punch, he was so appalled he was speechless. All he waned to do was go to Vermont and work on a farm for the summer. I decided right then and there that he could see Europe on his own or the government's time and I planned to use the money myself for a 20th Century "Grand Tour". As usual, I was about a year too late in my thinking. The bond had been cashed that fall to help pay off the carpenter in wolf's clothing at the back door. I must have known it at the time, but my memory is apt to be a little porous.

Sunday night, when we went to Slats', she greeted me at the back door in her best Katherine Gibbs manner. Her Mother was busy baking cookies and I asked her. "Are those for your daughter's lunch pail?" At the mention of pail, Slats turned pale, forgot all the dignity and polish she had acquired at K.G., and roared, "No lunch pails in my office, Smith, I take mine in a paper bag." I was very glad for this hot tip since Norm had come up from the cellar that very afternoon with a big black miner's lunch pail and had it scrubbed and ready for action. Norm and Slats' family both thought our going to Europe a figment of our imagination, so we went right into the living room and began looking at maps, travel folders, and we packed our suitcases out loud about five times. About nine, I was exhausted. She smirked and said, "You better, after al you are ten years old." That night I broke the news gently to Keith that I was about to become a "working mother". He said he didn't mind my getting healthy, but did I have to work too?

I said I had to work so I could go to Europe. He then asked if he and Punch would become juvenile delinquents while I was away at work. I asked, "Do you like Elvis Presley?" and he looked positively ill and said, "Heck no," so I told him I wasn't really going to worry about them becoming delinquents. Then came the really big question, "Don't you wish you were rich, Mom?", and I explained to Keith between rich and being poor is that the rich man can plan and the poor have to scheme. He said, "Goodnight, schemer, see you in the morning." He was so right.

Norm was really delighted that night when I requested him to awaken me at 6 the next morning. For years the poor man has been trying to run this establishment like an army camp, but there has been so much insurrection among the ranks that he finally gave it up as a lost cause. The idea of arousing me at six was the nicest prospect he had in years. I said, "Never mind the bugle, just call me," and his face fell.

Monday morning dawned about six hours earlier than I thought possible. It was too early for Dave Garroway, so I drank my coffee alone and at the ungodly hour of seven crawled out of my nice warm sack and began the painful process of dressing to go to work. I had decided on the grey flannel suite. What was good enough for Gregory Peck was good enough for me. Keith was in and out of my room full of questions such as, "Are you going to be a dictator?", which I assumed had something to do with taking dictation. I assured him that Slats was the dictator and that the power struggle wouldn't start my first day in the office. He wanted to know how much money I would earn and I told him that in our country today it was hard, if not downright impossible, to earn less than a dollar an hour. He seemed relieved about that. My breakfast was ready when I went downstairs and Norm was trying very hard not to look amused. I asked, "Didn't you bake any cookies for my lunch pail?" and he said, "I didn't even bake any for your lunch bag."

My muddy blue convertible was backed out of the barn and the motor was humming and neither Keith, nor Norm seemed overcome with emotion when I tore out the back door, ready to conquer the business world. In fact, at that very moment Norm was blissfully unaware of the fact that Slats' office was just a stone's throw form G. Fox, my favorite department store, which has raised more hell in Norm's civilian life than Rommel, the Desert Fox, did in his army life. I didn't know at the time myself that G. Fox was closed all day Monday.

What a break for everybody, and so my part-time working life began. It was nothing, really. Most of us are pretty well pleased with our jobs. It's the work we don't like.

THE NEW ADDITION

(1958)

In the normal course of events most children grow up, go away to school, and leave in their wake a house too large for just Mom and Dad. Not so with the Smith family, but please take note I did say normal. Now that Punch is at Pomfret and Keith home for just one more year, we are building on an addition which dwarfs the main house in size. Why? You might ask, what with two living rooms marked "His" and "Hers" and a perfectly good television room marked "Their's" are those fools building on? It's perfectly simple when you know this answer. When we moved into this house the Smith brothers were small, just Norm was large and I average. Now we have three giants dwelling here and when the big brothers come to visit, we fall all over each other before assigning rooms to various members of the family. I yearn to talk to all four of the Smith brothers at once without hooking up Norm's old army intercom system. I fully realize the high caliber the conversation will have to be to warrant at least ten percent of the construction costs. All I can really guarantee is that Norm will fast asleep in his favorite chair in "his" living room when we burn the mortgage in the new living room named "everybody's".

When anything of this nature happens in a small town, a great deal of speculation is the natural outcome. I will list for your amusement, I hope, a few of the weirder ones. First, it was said that the Smiths, (myself excluded), were of such an athletic nature, that we had visions of coaching the next Olympic basketball team in our gym. We laughed that one off. The next idea was that we were opening a rest home. Rest home indeed! Nobody around here ever gets a chance to rest, it isn't allowed. We keep busy, busy, busy all the time and nobody is allowed to rest. No, it isn't going to be a rest home. Jut ask the Haddick's, who go home to rest after a visit with the Smith's. This year they even took off Thanksgiving night so they could get some rest. A kennel perhaps? People have seen three Irish Setters cavorting about in the fields adjoining our place and when you see three setters in motion, it always looks like more.

A chicken house for Norm's favorite girls so he can readily get into production? No indeed, even without zoning we would never build a chicken house with a boxed-in picture window. Taking in borders, that's just an idle rumor. Now let me tell you what it really is. Just one large living room with a large bedroom over it so Keith can have one full year to play with the trains he never really has been able to enjoy before due to living in old houses with crooked floors, dirt bottomed cellars, cold attics, and a fussy Mother who refused to let the train stay on the T.V. room floor all one winter. The daytimes weren't bad, but if you ever had to get up at night, you couldn't make it in time because we never, ever leave lights on at night. The only reason there aren't any small Smiths is because someone gave me a small light to leave on in the nursery at night. Norm saw it and said, "That does it, no more babies in this house."

One thing we could do with less of these days is the advice of our friends. In the first place, they all advised us not to build, but now that we are, they are full of ideas which run the gamut from how to heat to how to decorate the interior. In fact, they have solved all our problems except how to pay for this enormous structure. What would we ever do without our friends. I ask what will we ever do with them. The bar looks like Lillian Roth stopped in before she started to bawl, and matters will get worse before they get better.

Another thing people always ask is, "Do you have a contract?" and we are forced to reply, "Hell no, we haven't even got an architect." That fact was more apparent than I like to think about the day before Thanksgiving. I had tooted over to Putnam to get a few things (next scene a twenty-eight dollar slip at the market place) to complete the Thanksgiving Day dinner. When I returned, the carpenters had left because the wind was blowing so strongly they couldn't stay up on their ladders. I'm glad they left because despite the gale, the north wall of the house looked like the Empire State building and they were still working their way up into outer space. Norm was alarmed when he reached home. The Haddick's were confused upon their arrival, but have learned over a period of years never to question us about anything so trite as a blank wall coming over a hundred feet in the sky. Norm just told them that Royal Barry Wills Smith had forgotten to tell the head carpenter just how high to go and he was obviously going to keep on until he had a hot tip from me. The day after Thanksgiving was devoted to bringing the wall down closer to earth and Norm was in his glory up high on the scaffolding, yanking off boards for nothing an hour which had cost $2.25 an hour to put up. Only cost, five carpenter's wages for a day to rectify this small error. From now on, even if the Smiths starve, I can't leave the job longer than five minutes a day.

As I write this, the roof is being raised. Tomorrow it might be razed, but today It looks good. This room that we were to sit in after our Thanksgiving dinner will be lucky if it gets sat in by Easter. The Haddick's will arrive tonight, and if Evelyn gets out with her binoculars to scan the skyscraper, she will be in for a rude awakening. It really looks like a house today, and we all know tomorrow never comes, so we're safe.

CHAPTER 7

Personal Letters within the Family

Phyllis Muriel Smith

The "In and Out" Letter from Grandfather to Phyllis

*Every summer from 1958 through 1971 The General was the Athletic
Director at Camp Indian Acres in Fryeburg. ME. Phyllis joined him the
first 3 years. After that Norm had his dachshund dogs as company. This is
one Phyllis considers classic Gen, and was written in 1962.*

Goodbye note to Nancy from Phyllis
*For several years, 1973-76, Punch and Nancy lived in Shrewsbury, MA., but
made Phyllis' home in East Woodstock their weekend headquarters.
Enjoying Elsie's Brook, cookouts and Phyllis' neat friends and fun parties.
This note was they moved once again, this time to Shelby, NC.*

Dear Nan,
  **Think of Tilly when you wear these. A little goodbye, and a great
deal of gratitude for all your help in getting ready for the Lion's party,
and for your own goodbye party. I can't begin to say how much I am
going to miss you, and mind having you and the girls so far away.**
            Love,
                Tilly

This "tongue in cheek" letter was written to Phyllis by Mr. McLean who purchased the Smith house in Huntsville, Pa in 1950, when Phyllis and Norm relocated to Woodstock, CT. It demonstrates the kind of light hearted humor their circle of friends enjoyed in that era, over 50 years ago.

LAW OFFICES
SHORTZ, JAMES & McLEAN
818 Miners National Bank Building
Wilkes Barre, Pa.

October 16, 1950

Mrs. Norman Smith
Hillside Road
Huntsville, R.D.,
Trucksville, Pa.

Dear Lady:

Please find enclosed herewith my check payable to your order, covering poultry, curtains, stools, etc. and WEATHER VANE in the amount of $244.50. I am also enclosing herewith a list of items covered by this check.

Your endorsement of this check will be my sufficient receipt for the payment of the items on the attached list and will forever close the question about the weather vane.

I am also enclosing herewith Hagerstrom Crafted catalogue. Inasmuch as we are now the owner of the WEATHER VANE we will not have any further use for the same.. You will note that the weather vane in question is No. 671 from page 4 of this catalogue, if I am correct, it being the small one 17" wide and 30" high as indicated under the heading "Weather Vanes" page 3 of the pamphlet. I am quite sure it is not the large 30" wide 40" high one.

Inasmuch as title to the weather vane and other articles purchases by the within check, passes with your acceptance of the check I am instructing the painter to lace a metal name tag bearing my name as the owner on the weather vane as soon as he can get his ladder up.

Now about the refrigerator – your remarks in connection therewith have cut me deeply. As you recall you did sign the agreement agreeing to include the refrigerator, inter alia, with the house for the price stated. You recall that the price stated was the price originally asked by you for the property. As our conversation at the time of the conclusion of the negotiations for the purchase of the house must have indicated to you I had looked into the value of your property, obtained expert opinion, and felt that the property had a real value of approximately $18,000. Recognizing a determined and stubborn woman when I see one, I realized the proper psychology for concluding the transaction would be to give in to you on the price that you are asking but to try and get some of the other items, which it would be necessary for us to purchase, thrown into the deal so as to get the net figure for the real estate down a little closer to something that I felt represented the real value thereof. You voluntarily entered into the transaction and the refrigerator is now mine – so in the future kindly be more considerate of my feelings.

At the time of your departure I will have a constable and a member of the S.P.C.A. on the premises with instructions to that you feed the poultry its last meal, that you do not leave Strayers' dog, that all articles that be reason of their fixation to the real estate has become blended therewith and title to which passes with the real estate, such as chandeliers, cupboards, wall fixtures, doorknobs and fences, weather vanes and all items of personal property specifically sold to us and included in the within list or included in the agreement for the sale of real property, remain on the premises t the time thereof. Any attempt at removal of any of these items or any further derogatory remarks about "the old man who chiseled you out of your refrigerator" will result in attachment of your person.

With all good wishes, I remain,

Sincerely, William S. McLean

This letter was received by Phyllis in February 1953. It was written

by a troubled friend, Nancy Felton Spencer. Phyllis wrote on the

envelope "I treasure it". As late as 2006, Keith and Phyllis would

visit Nancy at her home in Shrewsbury, VT. She and her children

all turned out to be quite functional happy people.

Dear Phyllis-Have you ever been tongue-tied? I would think that

the times that you were, were few and far between. Most human

beings suffer from the inability to express their thoughts clearly in

presence of another, and for this reason I am writing you a letter.

What I want to express to you today is common, old-fashioned,

garden variety, gratitude, on behalf of my four children, for being

so good to them, for doing all the things for them and with them

that their own mother doesn't do and should. Above all for enjoy-

ing the time you spend with them, and letting them know it. For

making them feel like people, wanted and respected for who

and

what they are. Going to Phyllis' house, is for them, a bright new

world, full of fun and laughter and useful knowledge. Their eyes

shine when they talk about you. After seeing you with my children,

I believe you truly love and enjoy them, it isn't an act. I envy you;

I am jealous for this capacity and someday intend to possess it if I

can.

I've learned a lot from you, about people, what fun they can be,

about laughing, about filling the day to day process of living with

meaning. I know that some people are really pleased to be alive,

and show it. Just being there for us has meant so much.

Here I am, having said almost everything I wanted to say and

still in the middle of the page. I don't seem to have the capacity

right now, to set the margins, for my letter or my life. Perhaps

taking a business course rather than psychotherapy would be

better for me and Jack and the kids.

Again, thank you before I close, sincerely, for your time and effort.

Thank you also for being our own "Mad Hatter". If someone didn't

try to put the dormouse in the teapot, we would all be too wrapped

up in ourselves to speak.

Affectionately,

Nancy

The "In and Out" Letter from Grandfather to Phyllis

*Every summer from 1958 through 1971 The General was the Athletic Director at
Camp Indian Acres in Fryeburg, ME. Phyllis joined him the first 3 years. After that
Norm had his dachshund dogs as company. This is one Phyllis considers classic
Gen, and was written in 1962.*

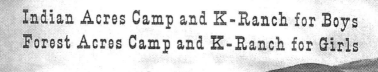

Indian Acres Camp and K-Ranch for Boys
Forest Acres Camp and K-Ranch for Girls

SEPARATE CAMPS — TWO MILES APART   WHITE MOUNTAINS   FRYEBURG   MAINE

DR. AND MRS. ABRAHAM KRASKER—DIRECTORS
WINTER HEADQUARTERS: 1125 THE PARKWAY—CHESTNUT HILL (67) MASSACHUSETTS. ASPINWALL 7-5112
NEW YORK OFFICE: 1100 PARK AVENUE—N.Y.C. (28) TRAFALGAR 6-5861

Sunday morning

Hi All:

Here it is Sunday morning. We are going to work
just this morning today. It has been very hot here with
a lot of sun. Dick Krasker has things very wekk organized.
I have been working on the two baseball diamonds with two
colored workers and one counselor. We out the weeds and ﬁﬂ;
stray grass from both diamonds and have had 8 loads of cla;
brought in and the oil man has been so we are far ahead of
any year I have been here.

Not many of the old counselors have arrived but quit
a few new ones and they all seem very capabble.

Snitch and Runt are OK. I drive the car each morning
up by the last cabin near the main building and leave it ﬀ
there all day. Snitch and Runst get out and run around whi
I am waiting for breakfast which we now have at 7:00 and ﬁ
then I put them in the car until after breakfast when I br:
them something and then I put them back in until the diffe
ent ones have movedout to their jobs and then I let them o
and they stay around until dinner time and I put them back
in where they stay again until the different ones move out
again and then I let them out and they stay until 4:30 wher
I taker a shower and then drive back to the cabin. They st
around in and out of the cabin until dinner time when I pu
them back in and then after di nner they are in and out
again. Snitch stays outside just in front of the cabin
until dark but Runt is in and out.

A couple f the counselors and the colored boys play
basketball every evening. We do n t have water in our
cabins in this area yet.

How is Bun coming along?

Dad

Over Thirty-Five Years of Nation-Wide Prestige

United States Senate

COMMITTEE ON FOREIGN RELATIONS

October 9, 1962

Mrs. Phyllis O. Smith
Sunnybank
East Woodstock, Connecticut

Dear Mrs. Smith:

I am happy to learn that you were recently admitted to American citizenship.

As one of your Senators in Washington, it is a pleasure for me to offer you my congratulations and a welcome to citizenship in this great land.

To be a citizen of the United States of America is a great privilege with great responsibility. As we enjoy the privileges of freedom and opportunity so must we do our best to preserve them.

If at anytime I can be of service to you, please feel free to call upon me.

With best wishes,

Sincerely yours,

THOMAS J. DODD

TJD:gf

237

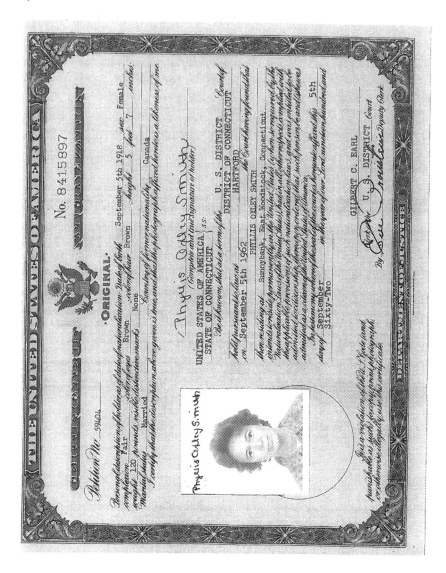

Goodbye note to Nancy from Phyllis

For several years, 1973-76, Punch and Nancy lived in Shrewsbury, MA., but made Phyliss' home in East Woodstock their weekend headquarters. Enjoying Elsie's Brook, cookout's and Phyliss' neat friends and fun parties. This note was written When they moved once again, this time to Shelby, NC.

Dear Nan,

Think of Tilly when you wear these. A little goodbye, and a great deal of gratitude for all your help in getting ready for the Lion's party, and for your own goodbye party. I can't begin to say how much I am going to miss you, and mind having you and the girls so far away.

Love,

Tilly

Excerpt for a couple of letters written by Kelly, 11, and Erin Smith, 10, granddaughters from Shelby, NC, in November 1979.

Dear Grandmother,

Sorry I haven written sooner. There are absolutely no excuses. I am spending the night with my other Grandmother as my parents are attending a Marine Corps Ball in Charlotte.

I look forward to your coming down for Christmas. I don't want anything except 1) Happy family and relatives and 2) Anything possible. I have a new puppy names Okra, named by mother from a dog in the book, "The Great Santini". I have my own world now because everybody started not to pay attention to me anymore.

Hope you move into your new house soon. I love you very much Grandmother. You don't have to write, but I hope you do.

Yours truly, I love you,

Er Bear, otherwise known as Erin Smith

Dear Grandmother,

How are you? House is your going? Hopefully those men will really get on their feet and get some work done! Mom said maybe you can come for Christmas. I really hope you can. I am at Mimi and Bob's house as my parents are at a Marie Corps Ball in Charlotte.

Thanks for sending me the smiley faces, because I wasn't feeling too good as e may have to move. We looked at a nice big house. Mom said not to worry because Dad can tell his company we won't move.

Mimi fixed chicken, rolls, gravy, sweet potatoes, which I don't care for, potato salad, peas, and tea. Yummy!

Hope your house gets done and soon. How are Keith and Miranda? I have been playing a lot of tennis lately. Erin has a new puppy, but she doesn't really care about him, so Mom says he is hers. We still have our cat Patches, but she is very old and may die soon.

Tell all my family up there hello, and come for Christmas. I love you very much and miss you a lot.

Granddaughter, Kelly

Phyllis Muriel Smith

After Christmas "Thank you" note from Nancy

Phyllis visited Punch and Nancy and their 3 daughters, Jennifer, Kelly and Erin for an extended Christmas vacation for over 30 years in St. Louis, Chicago and Shelby, NC.

From Shelby, NC   12/31/1979

Dear Til,
  Yesterday your package arrived and I'm still not over the surprise. It can't be said in a letter how I felt or am feeling now. The pearls are beautiful and I'll love wearing them, but naturally you're giving them to me is what is so special. I just wish you could be here.
  I think often about how fortunate I am (in many ways) but especially in having someone like you to care about me and my family. You have enriched our lives by being you. We all love you so very much and will be glad when your life can return to normal and you are no longer a displaced person.
  I called tonight in hopes of finding you at Keith and Miranda's, but wanted this note to be a special thanks for being my Mother-in-law. (And I'll thank Punch too!)
          Love,
          Nancy

Note: There images in this attachment, they will not be displayed. Download the original attachment.

Phyllis developed macular degeneration, first detected in the mid-1990's. This cryptic draft of a letter to an eye clinic in Boston, expressed her frustration in getting a clear diagnosis of her vision problems. We don't think this funny complaint was ever sent.

Dear Carolyn,

Forgive me for using your first name, but since I don't know your last,

(funny how only the doctors use their last names) as you are just the billing

clerk, it seemed more polite than to say "Hey you". The bill from Retina

Specialists arrived Friday, just in time to spoil what was to be a very

pleasant weekend. After the initial shock, I reread it, but it was still Greek

to me, or should I say Hebrew?

I journeyed to Boston the first time on the insistence of family and friends

who said I should get a second opinion. I would like to strangle the

person who thought that one up. Second opinion really means additional

expense. Several weeks ago I mentioned to my good friend Raymond

that I had not received a bill from you, and he said I eventually would, but

was too polite to say it would be a "whopper". Now a "whopper" to

Raymond, who owns a large chunk of south Boston, is not as much of a

shock as it is to me.

I think you should know you are dealing with someone who is not too many steps from spending the winter in a large cardboard box on the sidewalks of downtown Putnam, CT. Have you ever been to Putnam? Not even a hot steam grate in the sidewalk.

My first encounter of not too trange a kind, was with a Dr. Friedman. He admitted to his inner sanctuary, seated me in a chair, and rolled up a piece of equipment that must of cost the establishment a million dollars. I saw before me a chart with letters on it, like the eye exams in grammar school. As the lenses were changed, and the E's became B's, I lost interest and began a scenario in my mind's eye of Dr. Friedman, who exuded such an aura of success, I was fascinated. Married, a house in Brookline, tennis court, swimming pool, and probably three children, all extremely bright and attending the area's most exclusive private schools, in preparation for early acceptance into Harvard. A most attractive wife, who nipped in and out of shops on Newberry St. before meeting her svelte friends at Biba, as casually as I meet my chubby pals for lunch at Zip's. After the alphabet test, Dr. F asked about my reading habits. I told him my Puritan work ethic prevented me from reading during the day, but that I did indeed read at night. He asked where the light came from and I said overhead. He seemed disturbed and said that was very bad and that the light should come from the side and pointed to the lamp on my left. It was too tall to be a table lamp, and too short to be a floor lamp, and it was ugly, but Dr. F. recommended I invest in one. He said he would send me the ordering details, as I envisioned his wife's uncle in the Bronx who imported these ghastly objects from Japan, and making a tremendous profit selling to medical supply companies. On the way out Dr. F shook my hand and said "remember it takes a 60 watt bulb". I knew I had a 4 pack of 60's at home.

At the end of a long day and many tests later I saw Dr. Shapiro, or he saw me. Conversation proved to be a lost art, and I left with a prescription for drops and another for vitamin C and E. That was my first visit.

The second proved to be more of the same. Dr. F was most cordial, and we ran through the alphabet again. When I was leaving, I mentioned that I'd never received any info on the ready lamp. He said he make a note, and I thought, this place has more notes than the Boston Conservatory. I next saw Dr. S. who scanned numerous reports and told me he wanted to do another series of tests. This entailed a great many openings and closings of doors, and manila envelopes being placed in holders, before Dr. S recalled me to his office. By then it was 4:45 pm. I once again lowered my chin on a rest and placed my wrinkled brow on another rest. He said "let's do it" and commenced a ocular game. They literally shot tiny darts into my eyeballs, after dilation. I was ready to go play in Boston Traffic by that point, since nobody in that crazed driving city knew of my handicap.

Phyllis Muriel Smith

Seriously I will have to wait for my next visit to have this bill explained, and then I'll need to arrange something like a mortgage payment. I would really appreciate learning at that time what is wrong with my eyes, what can be done about them, and last but not least what is the prognosis? I await the answer to the $1411 question?

Most sincerely,

Phyllis M. Smith

P M S

April 3, 2006

Dear Clay and Marie,

The box of clothes you sent arrived and was much admired by all who saw the content. My favorite was the multi-colored velour slack and the enchanting brown velvet top. I can't wait to sally forth in that outfit. Thank you for all the clothes.

I am still waiting for a copy of your book. Jane said you thought you had enclose a copy in the clothes package. I did not find one though I thoroughly searched the box content. I know curiosity killed the cat so I better pull in my paws and stop asking you where my copy of the book might be. Life seems to go on here on much the same line. I see Keith quite often and Punch calls frequently. These cell phones certainly have altered our communication system.

I hope all goes well with you and Marie and I also hope your book will be a bestseller. Thank you for remembering me with all the nice clothes. I think six and eight are my best sizes. Hope you have a nice Easter and spring. Love to you both,

Grandmother

note courtesy of L. Davis

P M S

4/17/06

Dear Clay and Marie,

    I still go to my letterbox each day looking for Clay's book. Perhaps you can tell me who published it so next time one of my friends goes to Barnes and Noble, they can enquire about your book. I can't understand why I get so frustrated as each day goes by. Maybe I should resign myself to the fact of my ageing process. Anyway, I hope that your book-selling is going well.

    I am trying to do a bit of writing these days using a machine which records my stories

I never expect to get a book published but at least writing is a bit of an escape from my otherwise mundane life. Please let me know how things are going bookwise. I hope you and Marie had a pleasant Easter. I don't remember if Jane and Kim were coming or going to Florida. I hope to hear from you.

Love,
Grandmother

note: Kindness of L. Davis

September 5, 1988

Dear Phyllis:

It actually isn't the fifth of September just yet - but that's the date I wanted to use on this letter because it is meant to be a very special birthday greeting to you. You won't even get this by your birthday, because Labor Day is IT, and there isn't any mail delivery then. But you will know I am thinking of you and sending you love and wishes for much happiness, and "many happy returns of the day"--an expression from days gone by.

As your birthday nears, I've been thinking of all those days gone by. I met you for the first time just forty years ago...Labor Day weekend of 1948, when Bob and I drove to Trucksville from D.C. (he, from Quantico) to "meet the family." Among other things, there was a great birthday celebration/party for you, and I think it might have been your thirtieth. A milestone in anyone's life. A bummer for us females. A turning point, or so it seemed. I didn't know it then, for I was only twenty-two - a naive 22 - and when I think how different the next generation was at that age (Bob's and my children), I almost shudder to think what our grandchildren (Nikki and Christopher) might be doing when they reach age 22. Or age 30. Or maybe even age 15.

I remember the weekend well. I conjure up mental pictures of your house there - the built-ins and decor of Norma's former room...the large yard, and barn, and Dad Smith chasing after a rooster which might have had only one leg...his gathering eggs and making pancakes which were rich, rich, rich and smothered in maple syrup. I was intrigued by his calling you "Bun" - which Bob told me was short for Honeybun, and impressed with the obvious devotion to you of this huge, handsome man who had such an inner gentleness about him. I just knew that Bob was going to be like his Father, and it was true.

2

I remember well another holiday weekend, Memorial Day
in May 1949, when Bob and I were married. You and Dad
and two very young boys, Punch and Keith, arrived in
Athens in a black convertible with the top down. Was
there a dog with you then? You know, I don't remember
about that -- but most mental pictures I have from those
past years always include a big golden dog riding along
with its ears flapping in the breeze. Everyone in my
home town was so impressed with the Smith family...just
imagine a new bride being lucky enough to have someone
like you for her Mother-in-law. I can still "see" Dad
Smith and Bob sitting on the stairs of Thackery House
where we had the reception, having final man-to-man
conversation.

And so the years have swept by and the memories have
accumulated. Every visit of yours was special...from
Princeton Junction to Cherry Point (where you and Lila
stopped-coming and going to Florida one year) to Quantico
to Beaufort (where you came to take care of Robin and Clay
and Kim so that I could go to Europe and "follow the ship"),
to Gaeta in Italy (from whence you tootled up to France to
visit Jeanne and go biking with Princess Grace), to Athens
for Kim's wedding (straight from France, and where you were
a knock-out in an exquisite French creation), and all the
other times that were such fun for us all.

Such happiness. And such sadness. Marriages...divorces.
Births...deaths. Weddings...funerals. Has it been a
great and wonderful forty years since our first meeting,
or what???

You know, don't you, that I quote you? "Here's to Love."
"Never Explain, Never Complain." I also quote my Mother:
"Everything is Always Over." "To Thine Own Self be True."
"You're your own toad; you know how high you can hop." I
also quote Grandma Smith: "Worse, and more of it!" Sometimes I catch my children using these phrases, and it always makes me smile.

At Robin's wedding, I renewed my pride in the Smith clan.

3

You, the matriarch--again, in a knock-out of a gown.
Imagine looking like that! 'Way back there in 1949
when all the townsfolk were thinking how fortunate I
was in having a Mother-in-law like you, they just
didn't know the half of it.

So, Phyllis, this letter is not only to send love and
best wishes on your birthday. It is also to thank you
for being you...for always being there for us when we
needed you...for making us proud...for keeping me a
part of your life, even though we lost our beloved Bob
nearly twenty years ago. I take pleasure in all the
strong traits our offspring inherited from their Father.
Do you know what you and I have most in common? (Now to
quote my expression: "It takes one to know one.") We each
picked one wonderful man to be the Father of our children.

Go ahead, be seventy, if that's what the calendar says.
But to me you'll always be some nebulous age around
thirty or so...or ageless...or any age you feel yourself
to be. A very classy lady.

Have a happy birthday....

                    With our love,

                    Jane

Letter written by Jane to Phyllis in November 1990, just after Norma died of cancer. A newsy letter, mentioning many of the family members during that period.

Sunday, November 18th

Dear Phyllis:

Nice talking with you recently…just sorry that we had such sad news to discuss. I got the packet from Sam with Norma's memorial service bulletin, and copy of the obituary from the paper. He had called me to say he was mailing it – and also that the newspaper did not include Bob's name as a deceased brother, even though he and given it to them. He said they really have stringent rules about the information they will and will not accept. I think that he did just fine under the circumstances … not being at all prepared for supplying any information or even considering the possibility that he would ever have to.

On Veteran's Day, the city of Athens paid tribute to all their men who have lost their lives in Viet Nam – a dedication of a plaque on the Court House, which is really quite nice. There are 31 from here whose names are included – Bob among them, since we had taken this as our legal residence from the day of our marriage, needing a spot to vote and to buy license tags just to name a couple of reasons. A great number of people turned out for the ceremony, and then the VVA-100 chapter (local) hosted a reception for all the family members at the OU Inn. Again, quite nice. We were surprised by being presented with a replica of the plaque – each family – and I am sending you a copy of the special insert that was in our local paper covering the occasion. Copies of Robin's documentary tapes – "He's Only Missing" and the most recent one, "Seeking Answers" are being presented by us to the local libraries and the Historical Society, marking the occasion.

Also am sending you the copies of the articles from your papers about Clay's bike trip --- which he says is going to become an annual event with any and all invited to join in along the way, honoring the POWs and MIAs. Bob is the only MIA from this area, by the way – and tis is depicted on the plaque at the Court House.

Glad you have heard from Kim – am looking forward to seeing her in December when she comes home as I really do miss that lady. We try to talk on the phone each Sunday evening – would normally be calling her tonight, but she thought she might accept an invitation to go to Paris for the weekend. I am not just sure how her prospective employment is going to turn out --- seems as though it has taken for too long for the new restaurant in Avignon to take shape. It was programmed for this fall, then the end of this year, then January of 1991 – and Kim says that she doesn't foresee it being ready anytime in the very near future. Talking to her is like picking up on a weekly serial – stay tuned in for the next exciting chapter in the life of Kim Goes to France, Meantime, she is studying the language with the idea of keeping all her options open for whatever should come along. She has met many new friends...... which is something that comes easily to her .... And I know that she had been invited to share turkey with one young couple whom she has met. He is an architect for the Grand Hotel, and she was a dancer/entertainer at Lowe's in Monaco.

Phyllis – more later. Have a nice Thanksgiving – will be thinking of you and remembering what GREAT, GREAT FUN we had being there with you last year. I definitely want to do it again.

Much love, Jane

75ᵀᴴ BIRTHDAY LETTER

Phyllis saved this letter from her son Punch, written on the occasion of her 75th birthday in September 1993.

Dear Til – What do you say to your Mother on her 75th birthday? Particularly if she doesn't appear in body, mind, soul or spirit very much different than when she was 35! I guess a start would be congratulations on your obvious longevity, and let's plan to celebrate many more. You certainly have a bunch of memories of an eventful life. We wish you were closer to the Low Country Smith's, as we'd like you here to share our good times. Certainly a loud and heartfelt thank you from your son Punch is in order, for all that you have made possible through your love, encouragement and support. I could easily go on for pages, but the comfortable homes, the tasty means, the challenging schools and your being such a generous Grandmother, and caring Mother-in-law, are all part of my message.

Happy Birthday from all of us!

Love,

    Punch

80th Birthday

add
picture

80ᵗʰ BIRTHDAY   /198

Sometime in September, Somewhere in America

Dear Friends, Family, In-laws and Out-laws:

Always in search of adventure, and thanks to your kindness and generosity, I am off for 'round the world in eighty days' expedition. Fred Smith, world renowned fashion photographer, flew home from assignment in Tibet to capture this "parting shot" which surely will be featured in the travel section of the New York Times.

Further photos re likely to appear in such upscale lifestyle publications as Vogue, Harper's Bazaar, and W. Fred caught me emerging from the Chickering Hotel. For those of you not familiar with the more elite establishments of Connecticut, quiet corner, The Chickering is ideally situated a the heart of a modern transportation corridor (the railway tracks) in glamorous downtown Putnam, Ct.

In anticipation of an early start, I spent the first night of my incredible voyage here. You cannot imagine the luxury of this famed spa and I only hope that all my future accommodations are on a par with these.

You probably have noticed my new luggage, designed and manufactures in swank San Juan, PR. It provides the ideal protection for my newly acquired ensemble of designer clothes, calculated to show me at my very best during this far-ranging journey.

My going-away bouquet was provided by Frank Rogers and James Harvey (props), The Potted Palm in Providence, conveniently located next to Pot's Anonymous and Potted Parenthood. With bouquet in hand, luggage at the ready, I am perfectly prepared for my planned perambulations.

As the sign in the background confirms, Tilly likes to travel "lite." Sadly, this unanticipated journey will delay my enjoyment at home of the many delights and surprises you all provided during the recent celebration but, on my return I will enthusiastically indulge. Champagne and wine, Godiva chocolates and other goodies will guarantee that my new wardrobe will no longer be a "fitting" adornment. Freshly be-jeweled and be-jeaned. I will sally forth with friends to enjoy the diverse cuisines of The Golden Lamb, The Vine, Zip's Diner, Wendy's Burger King and KFC. This should fill my nights for some time to come. In the unlikely event of a nighttime indigestion or indiscretion, I can now fill the waking hours with books on tape, while listening for the "tempus fugit" songs of my modern cuckoo clock.

And with the stock market being, oh so "Dow Jonsey" just now, I am glad I can resort to my new "CD's" featuring such emerging and established groups as "The Carved Pumpkins," "Clinton and the Little Cigars" and "The Naked and the Dead."

If you wonder at this silly joviality, dear ones, I owe it all to you. For you, with your love and laughs, have helped to make the recent party and my passage into advanced middle age, an occasion to cherish and remember.

With love and gratitude,

    from Tilly

CHAPTER 8

Celebration of Life Service

Christ Church Pomfret, CT
August 8, 2009

Phyllis had two very close, "younger" friends – Nancy Weiss, who wrote this eulogy, and Mary Martin, who read it at this Service. Phyllis had "commissioned" Nancy, a gifted writer, years ago, to create something for her final service. Phyllis would have been most appreciative.

Phyllis and I became friends a long time ago. I was in my twenties and she was entertaining Rumanian engineers, who were sent to her by Sandy and Edith Rotival. I was invited because they spoke French and so did I, more or less. Their French was also lacking, so after copious drinks and many tasty hors d'oeuvres, we declared the evening a success and Phyllis and I were fast friends.

I admired her sense of style and taste. She could make a room, a garden, a sweater, a needlepoint pillow, a dish of cheese grits or her salmon mousse, look perfect, easy and utterly current. She liked to comb her hair by dragging her fingers through it and fluffing the top. She loved clothes and wore them with ease, accenting them with her trademark gold necklace. The necklace was just like the one owned by her friend, Elsie, as they both bought them at the same time and wore them everyday.

The sweaters she knitted for so many area children can still be found carefully preserved waiting for grandchildren to wear them or already pressed into use. For many Christmases, she invited a dozen or more of our children and to her home for a party. The children each received sweaters that Phyllis had knitted just for them. The parties were wonderful celebrations and a testament to the work Phyllis did constantly until her eyesight was gone.

Parties? Party was Phyllis' middle name. She loved parties more than anyone I have ever or will know. She liked to quote her friend, Sylvia Burton, who once said that Phyllis would go to a party in a Turkish toilet, if she were invited.

Phyllis, who somewhere along the line we began to call Tilly, I think because Keith called her that, was a bit like the late socialite Brooke Astor, whom she admired. Mrs. Astor went out to lunch and several parties every day and every night. Given the opportunity, Tilly would have chosen a similar path and kept up the pace. As it was, she took sleepy northeastern Connecticut and made it as lively and social as she could.

Who can forget the years when she and Richard Noren gave their annual shad roe party? Her Valentine's Day celebration was memorable for the way it cut through the dreariness of mid-winter as well as for the Bloody Mary's that still bring tears to my eyes in recollection as they were inordinately hot. Her East Woodstock house had the most beautiful deep yellow living room, but her modern home on West Road was where she really had the chance to show off her skills as an interior decorator, and a giver of memorable parties and beautiful gardens.

When her vision began to go, many of us took turns driving her to Boston to a specialist found by her dear friend, Ray Liston. She led me to believe the treatment took more time than they really did, so that those of us who accompanied her could shop or get our hair done.

One day when I went inside the doctors' office to get her, she handed me the paper work declaring her legally blind. I started to cry. It seemed so cruel that a woman who loved to read, do handwork, and saw beauty all around her would lose her sight. She patted my hand with her long skinny fingers, and said something like: "Well Miss Nan, we will just have to find something else for old Til to do. I don't want to get boring, you know."

We needn't have worried that she would get boring. While she bemoaned not being able to read, she loved books on tape, especially those Jane St. Onge got for her that corresponded with the selections of the no name book club, of which she was a proud founding member.

She liked being picked up by Mary Martin and taken to dinner at the Martin's home. After the book club meeting, at which she was an insightful, very witty participant, I would drive her home, enjoying even the trek to Creamery Brook as the drive gave us time to cover the million and one little things we wanted to discuss with each other. Such friendship!

Tilly loved to write. She once penned a weekly column in a newspaper, and wrote the best thank you notes anyone could ever receive. For one of her birthdays I thought I would get all her friends to select one thank you note from Tilly. I went through the stack I had randomly saved and chuckled often at her perfect comments. I wish I had saved everyone. Email will never equal her well-written commentaries on our lives here.

The last thing she wrote with me was a funny piece she entitled: "Coumadin Dreams". She was taking Coumadin and found a side effect was amazing, vivid dreams. By this time, she couldn't see, so she dictated the story to me while I typed on my computer. The story was classic Tilly: witty comments on George Bush, 18-wheelers and thoughts about Howard Dean. We wrote it and she distributed it to family and friends.

I keep a photo of Tilly, called our Town & Country shot, near my desk. It was taken at Easter long ago and we both look pretty good in it. I get a lump in my throat when I see it as it reminds me that I have lost one of the best friends I will ever have. Many of you certainly feel the same way about her. She was one of a kind, a gracious, witty, lively, thoughtful, accomplished woman, who would look around this gathering and think: good, glad my friends are here. Hope they have a little party afterward.

Phyllis Muriel Smith

Son Punch's words of farewell.

Phyllis was a witty lady, of very few, well chosen words, and a little self-effacing. If she were standing next to me today, I'd help her picture the large crowd gathered to say goodbye. And she would probably say, "Oh Punch, they just heard Chris Dodd was holding a town hall meeting"!

She'd ask me to keep it short and light, and not to antagonize too many Democrats.

Tilly spent her last 18 months at the Palms, a cheery facility with good food and a pleasant staff, just 3 miles from our home in Mt. Pleasant. She enjoyed independent living, a small apartment, and going down twice a day for meals. It was very important to her, and her biggest fear was going to the Nursing Home section. Her ability to "live independently" was made possible by our oldest daughter Jennifer, who took her shopping, to doctor visits and to get her hair cut. Nancy helped out by helping with showers, doing her laundry, and arranging frequent visits to our home. My contribution was managing her medicines, handling her paperwork and joining her and her friends, Florence and Victoria, for a couple lunches per week. She especially enjoyed, as I did, the Sunday Brunch. Her staple was cream cheese and salmon on bagels.

She listened to 8-10 books on tape per week, and kept her TV tuned to CBS, and radio to NPR. She never was confident switching channels!

Our family has received numerous sweet notes of sympathy, many from you here today. In closing, allow me to read excerpts from a tender note from Arlene and Lenny, fellow residents.

Arlene and Len Fries
The Palms, Suite 375
937 Bowman Road
Mount Pleasant, S.C. 24946

Dear Punch,

News of your Mother's passing was very sad for a lot of people here at the Palms.

Though your Mother had trouble seeing, she sure developed a lot of respect and affection from those who live here and observed her daily, smiling gently, and making her steady trip to her table.

We had the pleasure of seeing her very often in the dining room. It would be our pleasure to walk to her table and exchange a few words and smiles. There were times when I would watch her try to pick something up with her fork and it would be empty! It was a sad sight – but, she handled it with dignity and acceptance.

A pleasing high light of her departure…surely in heaven…she will see beauty again!

Punch, we truly cared for your Mother….our dear friend…..Phyllis Smith.

Our friendship started when, on a few occasions, finding her way to her table was difficult…but easy for us to see. I would jump up to take the front of her walker and lead her to an appropriate table…and from time to time, get something for her.

Here is the part that really brings tears to my eyes (Punch's comment)

Funny, but when I did things for her….it made me feel good too!

HOW WE WILL MISS THIS LOVELY, DIGNIFIED, SWEET, GENUINE LADY!

From son Keith and daughter-in-law Miranda

Keith and I would like to extend our warmest greeting and appreciation to Phyllis' beloved Family and all her special friends gathered to celebrate her life.

The death of a loved one is often perceived as being an End. Our physical bodies are not what we are; the Spirit and Soul are the reality. We all experience a painful and often overwhelming sense of loss when our loved one is no longer with us physically.

When my dearest friend and Mother crossed over ten years ago, I felt there was a hole in my heart where my soul used to be. With time, I came to realize that her presence and love was just as close to me as she was on this earth.

This healing and transformation takes time. Don't let anyone try to convince you that there isn't terrible pain and also that your conflicting emotions can be quickly resolved. It's okay to be very sad and it's more helpful for people to talk to us about it, rather than pretend that a significant change has not occurred.

Tilly taught me a great deal – too much to detail. For example, I didn't know how to cook when I married her son, Keith, 35 years ago. Tilly's fantastic cooking and her eye for beautiful presentation was somewhat daunting to me at first, but she was generous in sharing her cooking hints and talent. I recall her incredible black bean soup, her creative salads, and of course, garlic bread baked with Rosemary!

Tilly's amazing home decorating expertise was a daunting task to emulate, as was her style and elegance in the way she presented herself.

She made entertaining look easy, it isn't always easy for some of us, but she gave me confidence to do it. Martha Stewart could learn plenty from Tilly in that department.

When I think of the words, "For the beauty of the earth and the wonder of the flowers", she instantly comes to mind. It was a cruel loss for her to lose a great deal of her eyesight, but she dealt with it with her usual grace and acceptance.

The pleasure of getting to know Phyllis had another incredible benefit – knowing her wonderful husband, General Norman Smith, or Cuffy, as we fondly called him. Cuffy and I enjoyed watching many a Red Sox game upstairs in his TV room at their East Woodstock home,

Sunnybank. There was always a dog on Cuffy's lap during a ball game, though not much conversation was flying around, those times are very dear memories in my heart.

Tilly had a great sense of humor, a quick wit, and very sharp mind. She, as many individuals of her generation, has crossed over now, but their positive imprint on all our lives is indelible.

We are all better for having Phyllis in our lives.

Memories from Grandson Clay

My grandmother encouraged me to write, so I did. To be unable to find humor, or to joke, is truly a loss of a gift, one that could be either inherent or mimicked simply given from one to another. To laugh is to remember a gift from my both my grandparents.

My Grandmother was never what a grandmother was thought to be. She was truly advantaged. Jet set, if you will, important to us.

A creator of stories, written and spoken ... some true and some invented, but never the less all high-quality works of one who truly loved to express with wittiness. Humor is the building block of our family. A rough foundation made up of misfortunes, but always smoothed out with a sense of humor.

We laughed until tears streamed down from both eyes. Early on, eyes that could see, later, eyes that could only easily cry... but didn't.

A critic would critique as an outsider, one who was not in on the gag would join in, swept up with the spirit of our family, a pleasure to be in the midst of us at family gatherings.

Then we all gathered at Phyllis favorite winery, Sharpe Hill.

CHAPTER 9

Phyllis The Philanthropist

$ Phyllis the Philanthropist $

There once lived a lady named Tilly,
Who thought spending money was silly,
So before you could Google, she became very frugal.
To phone long distance, was not in her existence.
Because there was less for old Ma Bell, soon her account did really swell,
And now the rest of us will all live well.

THANK YOU

Phyllis Muriel Smith

Memorial fund established at Marianapolis

ENDOWMENT WILL SUPPORT ATHLETIC DEPARTMENT

BY ADAM MINOR
VILLAGER STAFF WRITER

THOMPSON — In an effort to support the school's athletic program and memorialize a friend, a Marianapolis Preparatory School alum has taken it upon himself to start a fund to do just that.

The "General" Norman W. Smith Memorial Fund, dedicated to a former teacher, has been created to support Marianapolis athletics, and ease pressure on the school's general fund.

"It's a memorial fund in 'the Gen's' name, which is an endowment," said Joseph Scanzillo, former Marianapolis student and a member, of the Board of Directors of the Trinity Foundation, the organization that runs Marianapolis. "The purpose of the endowment is something that will last in perpetuity for the benefit of the athletic department at Marianapolis. It's not a one-time thing — it's an ongoing thing from which the athletic department will be able to annually take some of the proceeds from the fund and support the athletic programs here."

Smith — or "The Gen" to Scanzillo — taught at Marianapolis from 1958 until his death in 1978, and was also a coach of various sports at the school.

Scanzillo attended Marianapolis from 1965 to 1966 as a post-graduate student from

Dedham High School in Dedham, Mass. He said he credited Smith for his success there.

"'The Gen' was a very special man," Scanzillo said. "He was one of my very favorite people while I was here as a student. He had an amazing ability to relate to young people, not only from a coaching perspective, but also from a human perspective. He had a great sense of humor, and a great sense of insight."

Smith was born in 1902 in Burrillville, R.I. He graduated from Dean Academy in Franklin, Mass., and later, with a degree in mathematics from the University of Rhode Island (URI) in 1925. At URI, he was a successful football, baseball, basketball and track athlete, and after school, coached at Wyoming Seminary in Kingston, Pa. He served in the Army in World War II, participating in campaigns in Europe, and Africa. In 1958, he joined the faculty at Marianapolis.

Although he never achieved the rank of general in the military, Marianapolis students tagged him with the nickname anyway.

"A lot of the priests, when I was here, had nicknames," Scanzillo said. "Everyone had a name, sort of like 'Fonzie.'"

Forty years after he graduated, Scanzillo found himself a member of the Trinity Foundation Board of Directors, and decided to start the fund in honor of "the Gen."

"It was time to pick up the torch and do so thing about it," he said. "For many year knew that Marianapolis was a turning po in my life. It's crystal clear to me that if I not come here — if I was not accepted he and given the opportunity to change wha had been doing — that I would have just c tinued on the path I was on. Marianapo clearly provided me the opportunity to [change]. By the time I graduated fr up dramatically, and I had several coll opportunities. I would not have had t without my experience here."

Scanzillo added another reason behind memorial fund was knowledge of school's need for upgrades and renovati By creating a separate fund for athletics, school wouldn't have to worry about us general fund money to support it.

The creation of the fund was made officia a Board of Directors meeting Monday, Dec.

"It's a wonderful and generous gift," s school Headmistress Marilyn Ebbitt. "It' gift that celebrates the power that teache coaches and mentors can have on developi young people's lives."

The fund, Scanzillo said, must reach a m imum threshold of $50,000 before funds c be withdrawn, but said the threshold can altered depending on the needs of the scho

"My hope is that once t establishment of the fund made aware to the public, the will be support of the fund, a donations, so that it will reac level that will ensure longevity and health," he sa "I am hoping that this is ju one of many similar types memorial funds that will mer rialize other deserving peor in the future."

The funds can be used at the d cretion of the school's athle director, Eric Gustavsc Hopefully, Scanzillo said, t General Smith fund will inspi similar funds to start up.

"I could rattle off names other deserving people who I a hoping to establish funds for," said. "It was easy for me to pi 'Gen,' because he is one of t special people that should memorialized. He was a wonde ful man, and if anyone is to memorialized, it should be sor one like him."

To donate to the "Genera Norman W. Smith Memori Fund, call (860) 923-9565, vis www.marianapolis.org, or mai checks payable to Marianapol Preparatory School, restricted the General Smith Fund.

Courtesy photo

The "General" Norman W. Smith Memorial Fund was announced at a Marianapolis Preparatory School Honors Convocation on Nov. 20. From left, Smith's son, Keith, his wife, Phyllis, the fund's creators, Joseph Scanzillo and his wife, Jo, and Headmistress Marilyn Ebbitt.

Adam Minor may be reached . (860) 928-1818, ext. 112, or by e-m at adam@villagernewspapers.cor.

Phyllis Muriel Smith

THE RECTORY SCHOOL
528 POMFRET STREET
PO BOX 68
POMFRET, CONNECTICUT 06258-0068

August 26, 2009

Mr. Norman W. Smith, Trustee
Phyllis M. Smith Revocable Trust
116 Hyer Street
Mt. Pleasant SC 29464

Dear Mr. Smith:

I was deeply saddened to hear of your mother's death and would like to express my sincere sympathy to you and your family.

I understand Phyllis was a good friend of Rectory. I am sorry I didn't have the opportunity to meet her.

On July 31, 2009, The Rectory School received the bequest from the Phyllis M. Smith Revocable Trust. This gift will be applied to the 2009 Annual Fund and *will be designated to Campus Beautification Projects.*

I know how difficult this time is for you and the rest of your family. Our thoughts are with you.

Sincerely,

Fred Williams

Frederick W. Williams

Your family's generosity is greatly appreciated and Rectory will use this money wisely to honor your mother's legacy. Rectory's campus is one of its greatest assets and your gift will enhance our beautiful setting.

Gift Received: $10,000.00

This letter is your receipt to acknowledge your contribution and the fact you were not provided with any goods or services by The Rectory School in consideration, in whole or in part, for your contribution. Your contribution to The Rectory School Annual Fund has been received and gratefully acknowledged.

OFFICE OF THE HEADMASTER • TEL. 860-928-7759 • FAX 860-963-2355

270

August 12, 2009

Mr. Norman W. Smith
116 Hyer St
Mt. Pleasant, SC 29464

Dear Punch,

Please accept my sincere condolences on your mother's passing.

As you may know, your mother was one of Pomfret's most loyal supporters. We are very grateful for her thoughtfulness in including Pomfret School in her estate plan.

My thoughts are with you and your family.

Sincerely,

Bradford Hastings '68
Headmaster

BH:jm

398 Pomfret Street • PO Box 128 • Pomfret CT 06258-0128
860-963-6127 • Fax 860-928-1034
www.pomfretschool.org

Phyllis Muriel Smith

John H. Shafer
Vice President of Advancement

570-270-2140
Fax 570-270-2199
jshafer@wyomingseminary.org

WYOMING SEMINARY
founded 1844

August 3, 2009

Norman W. Smith, Jr.
116 Hyer Street
Mount Pleasant SC 29464-5009

Dear Norm:

I am writing to express the gratitude and appreciation of everyone associated with Wyoming Seminary and to acknowledge the recent bequest of your mother, Phyllis M. Smith, in the amount of $10,000. In accordance with her wishes, this bequest will be added to the Robert N. Scholarship Endowment Fund. I thank you for your prompt and efficient handling of this matter as the trustee of your mother's estate. From our recent phone conversation, I know you are pleased she has earmarked her gift to the scholarship fund your family established in 1999 in memory of your brother. I would ask you to share our gratitude with your siblings and the other members of your family.

Wyoming Seminary has been able to provide a meaningful educational experience for 165 years due to the generosity of alumni and friends who include the School in their estate plans. Your mother is an integral part of this group of forward thinkers who help make a quality education possible for future generations of students.

I want you to know how much her gift means to the school. Thanks again for all you do for Wyoming Seminary in so many ways. Please know your many friends at Sem at thinking about you and your family and remembering you in our prayers. As we discussed on the phone, your mom lived a rich and full life. Best wishes from the campus.

Sincerely,

John H. Shafer
Vice President of Advancement

COLLEGE PREPARATORY SCHOOL
201 NORTH SPRAGUE AVENUE
KINGSTON, PENNSYLVANIA 18704-3593
WWW.WYOMINGSEMINARY.ORG

IT WAS NOTHING!

MARIANAPOLIS PREPARATORY SCHOOL

August 17, 2009

Phyllis Smith Trust

Mr. & Mrs. Norman Smith
116 Hyer Street
Mount Pleasant, SC 29464

Dear Mr. & Mrs. Smith,

Thank you for your thoughtful gift to Marianapolis Preparatory School Annual Fund. Your gift of $ 10000 will enable us to offer our students strong academic and co-curricular programs which, in the spirit of the school's Mission Statement, will empower them to meet the demands and challenges of a rapidly changing and morally complex world.

Marianapolis has been fortunate in maintaining an experienced faculty and in attracting many qualified students to our school. Opportunities for students and teachers to enhance the learning process by a judicious use of technology have taken a quantum leap in the past few years. We are pleased to see our students succeed in the fields of the performing arts, publications, athletics, and college placement.

Your contribution reinforces a tradition of philanthropy and involvement in the life of the school by alumni, parents and friends and sows the seeds for a beautiful and bountiful harvest of educational opportunity for generations to come

The Marianapolis community is grateful for the spirit and substance of your contribution.

Gratefully,

Marilyn S. Ebbitt
Headmistress

Charles Baron, P'93 & P'95
Trinity Foundation - Vice Chairman

Gift Receipt

Marianapolis Preparatory School affirms that neither goods nor services were provided as consideration of this contribution. The amount of this gift constitutes a deductible contribution in its entirety.

Donor: Norman Smith
Gift Date: 08/17/2009
Gift Amount: $ 10000.00